SCHEMING IN THE
DARK

MATTHEW STRIDIRON

D1598591

ISBN: 978-0-578-29944-0

FOREWORD

"I am honored to give my blessings and write this appreciative note for this book. This important and entertaining look into the broken machine that is public education. An insider's look at how politics and favoritism rule the day, when it comes to school districts like Newburgh. I fully support and urge you to read this first hand account. We often focus, in our society, on race and privilege, important topics no doubt. But we don't talk about how much power these school districts have and how willing they are to throw that power around at their discretion, while the boards of education are all too willing accomplices. This book provides a fascinating peek inside, it's well worth the time."

RICHARD DESIDERIO
former Newburgh Free Academy teacher

TABLE OF CONTENTS

Acknowledgements and Dedications vii

1 Before We Begin: An Introduction to Newburgh 1

2 A Call To Action 11

3 Children Caught In The Middle 29

4 Guarded Lives 45

5 A Path Less Travelled 57

6 Unleash The Kraken 73

7 Shattered 93

8 Searching For Answers 131

9 Looking Up to Family 161

10 Impartial Justice 175

Postface 189

Author's Note 191

Resources 193

ACKNOWLEDGEMENTS AND DEDICATIONS

This book would not be possible without the great support that many people and groups offered me during the most challenging, yet most enriching, parts of my life.

I'd like to first honor the Mclymore Foundation with thanks for really pushing me to start writing a book. Although this book is not the one I originally planned to write, this one has the power to change many more people through its themes of family and endurance.

The Newburgh P-TECH program's staff should also receive praise for proving that I can always strive to do better, even when I think I can't.

My father, through his service as a school board member, showed me what it takes to lead while under immense social and political pressure. I understand that making good decisions isn't always easy. While people may initially disagree with your actions, they don't know what went into your decision making. What matters is that you made your choices for the right reasons.

The school teachers and administrators who I interviewed for this book edited some of the chapters so that they would not only explain a complex problem in great depth from a neutral perspective, but also foster political dialogue about the issues. Despite how this book was originally an autobiography, they enabled *Scheming In the Dark* to also focus on community.

My classmates who I befriended during my senior year of high school gave me positive memories that I always think back to. Over these last few years, life has been rough on everyone. Still, those memories have kept me strong when I too would have been knocked down.

Lastly, I'd like to thank a former mentor of mine from the Matriculate program for showing me how to really write good stories. No matter how powerful a personal story is to you, it may not be as powerful to others. Writing about those events well is not just about describing what happened. It's also about how the story comes off and the impression you give to readers. Thanks to him, I know that my point of view isn't always the whole story. I've done my best to include multiple perspectives using whatever means I felt were reasonably necessary while also keeping that narrative component intact.

1
BEFORE WE BEGIN:
AN INTRODUCTION TO NEWBURGH

Newburgh, New York, occupies a special place in America's history. It was the location of George Washington's headquarters during the last year and a half of the Revolutionary War.[1] It was where he subsequently refused to accept a crown as the country's first king.[2] With the right leadership, the city was built by good people in the years to come. As more mansions were built along the bluff overlooking the Hudson River, my hometown became a showcase of Victorian architecture and a site to explore new forms of practical living and country home design.[3] Newburgh attracted the best architects and craftspeople in America, making the city a great tourist attraction. While steamboats from New York City brought visitors who found Newburgh to be the perfect retreat from urban living, Newburgh's residents made their way to New York City to design public parks.[4] By 1900, we became more independent and transformed into a solid working-class community. Machine shops that initially manufactured boilers and generators to keep the steamboats up and running turned into garment factories that were led by some of the world's largest producers of work clothes. People came from near and far to shop at our bustling downtown district, which we always called Broadway. For comparison, think of Broadway as a two-mile long shopping mall. Newburgh's historical records show my hometown had five movie theaters, two roller skating rinks, fifteen auto showrooms, dozens of barbershops, over fifty clothing stores, sixty-six restaurants, sixteen jewelry stores, and twenty-five clothing manufacturers at the time, something pretty impressive for a "small" upstate town.

Even as remnants of Newburgh's beauty persist in its architecture with the still-stunning views of the Hudson, its decline was surprisingly dramatic by the 1960s. My hometown lost its touch not because of the failing economic times or the emergence of something new, but by the sudden destruction of what made us great to begin with. Around that time, many hard-working residents left the city. The collapse of the manufacturing base left Newburgh without an economy to support itself.[5] Rather than encourage new, skilled laborers to move in and rebuild the economy, my city relied on federal funds to rebuild itself. In order to qualify for these funds, the city had to designate certain areas as slums - which are zones categorized as undesirable and in a poor state of repair. Based on accounts from the City of Newburgh, however, many of the city's "slums" looked like "well-maintained," historically significant buildings. Some of the buildings had stores that people sold goods in. Still, around 1,300 good-quality buildings were demolished over the years. The destruction annihilated downtown's commercial district. Nine well-preserved streets were also plowed under, including Clinton Square, a triangular confluence of streets with a bronze statue of George Clinton (one of New York's greater heroes during the Revolutionary War). The remaining law-abiding, working class citizens who initially had no plans to leave their homes moved out either because their taxes were going through the roof or because their home was about to get torn down by a wrecking ball.

In spite of how we sit on a goldmine of historically important American heritage that can nourish the spiritual and intellectual life of our community, one newspaper described urban renewal as the lead factor which caused Newburgh to morph into "a shell-shattered town of some gigantic war."[6] Because Newburgh lost so much, the city continued to decline. During recent years, Newburgh repeatedly made it to the list of America's fifty most dangerous cities.[7] My town has even been called the "Murder Capital of New York."[8] In the late evening, after the street parties conclude and the lights turn off, you can see the frightened eyes of people looking out for gunshots coming from gang wars and riots. The sirens of paramedics blare louder and louder as they near the scenes of the crimes. Most of us understand the dangers of crime and that our infrastructure isn't in the best condition, but beyond that, many people don't fully understand the poverty they live in today and the efforts of those on the school board trying to help them.

The Newburgh Enlarged City School District (NECSD) is the school district within Newburgh. Its Board of Education (BOE) is a body consisting of nine elected officials who are supposed to directly oversee the superintendent's management of the day to day operations within the schools. They work with the Central Office administrators, who are officials like the superintendent that oversee the schools from a district-level perspective. The NECSD is not your typical school district, given the city's history. Given that many businesses left the area after the 1960s, the district (by default) became one of the largest employers in the area. The local manufacturing jobs transformed into teaching services, which is why we haven't had many other jobs in the area ever since aside from the small restaurants nearby. That's what makes my community's school board politics so influential in the region. The weekly-held meetings at the Newburgh Free Academy Library are the hub of the city's economic life. Academic performance and attendance records are akin to the City Council's finances and budget. When the schools perform poorly, the New York State Education Department (NYSED) - the state governing body for education - does not provide funding to the district. Without that funding, Newburgh's economy will undoubtedly decline. It is always essential that the administrators allocate these funds appropriately.

My father, as of the time of this book's publication, currently serves on the BOE and has done so since 2014. The title he holds is won through a local election every three or four years. Despite the challenges that come with becoming a board member, he chooses to run for re-election because he really wants to better the education of local students. Even before he ran an election campaign for the position, his constant presence in the community transformed him from an outsider with no political experience to a neighborly friend in the eyes of his peers. He is a virtuous man with many supporters. Together, we know information about the city, its people, and their fascinating stories spanning back forty years. I wanted him to help write a few chapters since he knows so much information that I don't, and he gladly agreed. We would meet up every weekend for a phone call to check on his progress. Yet as the weeks went by, he got nothing done. In recent years, he's seen his morale drop. Certain people who are also interested in politics on the school board stole his excitement for serving on the BOE. My father's opponents made it clear that they do not want him on the board. Out of the 150 re-election signs he purchased, 100 were stolen. One of my brothers and I found them publicly visible outside an old abandoned house near a local middle school. At one point, my family coated hot sauce and chili powder mixed with vaseline, a tar that is almost impossible to wash off your hands, onto the back of the signs to discourage theft. His critics, amazingly, still took them down. Imagine all of the vaseline they had on their hands!

From what I've seen, you need to be tough and take pain like a sponge in Newburgh. The biggest challenge I had when writing *Scheming In the Dark* was making the book's story relevant to a broader audience. How do I make a story about New York relevant to the people living in other places? To answer this question, *Scheming In the Dark* consists of two components that are interwoven with one another: a narrative component and a community component. I made part of this book into an autobiography. What my father and other older family members experienced as I grew up is by far the biggest factor which convinced me that a book needed to be written because they've sacrificed so much for my brothers and I. My family members used to stay up until midnight since they had lots of energy. Nowadays, the lights die out four hours early. Some of them lost their enthusiasm, so I want to make sure things change for the better. As they slept, I sacrificed two entire summers bunkered down in a basement during a world health pandemic to draft up chapters. I worked from eight in the morning to midnight. I deviated from my other hobbies during two school years to put an acceptable amount of time into this writing project, hoping to perfect what I've worked on for so long. If you ever read *A Long Walk to Water* or

Persepolis, this book is similar in that the narrative portion focuses on family, community, loss, resilience, and survival. This is a story about an impoverished neighborhood told by children who grew up there, and the effects of the town's political strife largely affects them rather than the adults. At the same time, this book is distinct for how the social problems are much more relevant to you, the reader. You'll get to see the impacts of poverty and local politics are on the city's residents, even if they don't care about either. The one thing I remember most about my book announcement is all of the positive support I received when people saw the book trailer. My mother and brothers were ecstatic when I showed them the trailer on Easter Sunday. The NECSD's employees told my father and I they were "excited" and "thrilled." One person outside the country who I showed the trailer to called my book "revolutionary." For a book about politics, this unity is rare. They recognized this book as the first real attempt to fix Newburgh's problems since the 1960s.

Despite how there are very personal stories in this book, my goal is to remain as objective as possible. To encourage anonymity of individuals, no names will be mentioned. I want to talk about the story itself. As I wrote this book, I wanted to obtain multiple perspectives using whatever means I felt were reasonably necessary. If I did not reach out to certain people for comment directly, it is because their points of view were already expressed in some sort of dispute or legal hearing that's already been settled (especially in the book's more personal stories). In fact, much of what you're about to read is documented by these court depositions, reports, and newspaper articles. Endnotes appear at the end of each chapter for anyone interested in learning more. There's no reason to take what I'm saying with a grain of salt. Some of the evidence that I use also comes from social media posts, recorded videos, text messages, and recorded interviews that I administered with educators. Regardless of whether you own an e-book or a physical copy, you need to access this evidence using the book's special Google Drive (link at end of chapter). What those documents (which I expect to remain anonymized) describe should be something that brings people together, not tears people apart. It should encourage the citizens of cities like Newburgh to take pride in restoring their cities to their former glory.

The remaining chapters will bring you through four years of my life, starting from my freshman year of high school when my father served on the BOE all the way to the summer before my freshman year at college. I appreciate you for taking the time out of your day to understand what I have to say. You could be doing other things. Instead, you're taking the time to read an in-depth analysis of the problems that exist within public schools, the very institutions that deal with millions of children each and every year. While I describe my hometown in great detail, this book is not a case study. *Scheming In the Dark is designed to change the way you see education and justice systems in their entirety, not just in my hometown.* The book is divided into three arcs. Arc 1 sets up the context for Arc 2 and 3, the main narrative (semi-autobiographical) story, by showing you exactly what the people in my hometown are struggling with on a daily basis and why it's so important for them to get the help they need. After the next chapter, which goes into some of these problems, Arc 1 is meant to be somewhat formal in tone. Some of the content comes from interviews with local teachers who I interviewed for several hours because they wanted to see a change in public education. In Arc 2, the book offers its narrative and more personal story. In Arc 3, the book keeps this narrative tone while bringing Arcs 1 and 2 together. You can clearly see I wrote about a hard, yet interesting, topic. If you are not interested in reading *Scheming In the Dark* based on everything I laid out so far, I encourage you to stay for at least two or three chapters. By the time you reach the last page, you will have a better understanding of local, state, and national politics than you were probably expecting. Now, let's dive into the actual book.

Google Drive folder can be located at scheminginthedark.com.

If you cannot see or read the text off of one of the pictures within the book, please look at the Google Drive.

Important Note: As of December 1, 2021, I verified that all of the links in the endnotes for each chapter work. However, some of them have since been disabled by the respective sources. This book frequently cites stories from the Times Herald Record. To my knowledge, they recently merged with another newspaper firm. This acquisition may have caused some of their links to malfunction. I tried to verify whether this may be the case, yet the newspaper did not respond to my inquiry. Thankfully, I saved all of the Times Herald Record articles that I am citing to an external drive in advance. If any links belonging to the Times Herald Record or any other newspaper malfunction when you access them, please reach out to the respective source.

CHAPTER ENDNOTES

1   Lynn Woods, "Lost Newburgh: The Tragedy of Urban Renewal, Part 1," *Newburgh Restoration*, January 17, 2018, https://newburghrestoration.com/blog/2018/01/17/lost-newburgh-the-tragedy-of-urban-renewal-part-1a/

2   Ibid

3   Ibid

4   Ibid

5   Ibid

6   Cher, "Lost Newburgh: The Tragedy of Urban Renewal, Part 3," *Newburgh Restoration*, January 19, 2018, https://newburghrestoration.com/blog/2018/01/19/lost-newburgh-the-tragedy-of-urban-renewal-part-3/

7   Bobby Welber, "Hudson Valley City Among 'Most Dangerous' in US, 3 From New York," *Hudson Valley Post*, January 27, 2021, https://hudsonvalleypost.com/hudson-valley-city-among-most-dangerous-in-us-3-from-new-york/

8   Patrick Radden Keefe, "Welcome to Newburgh, Murder Capital of New York," New York, September 23, 2011, https://nymag.com/news/crimelaw/newburgh-2011-10/

ARC ONE

2
A CALL TO ACTION
2015 - 2016

E very school day began around seven in the morning inside a white-painted hallway covered with retired Spanish and biology textbooks stacked on top of one another. A black divider was positioned ahead to indicate that the long line of students arriving through this hallway should break up into two separate lines. On this particular day, I was able to reach the front of the right row quickly and get into the actual building. Welcome to my high school, which people like to call Newburgh Free Academy (NFA) North. My friends were already hanging out downstairs outside the door to our first class of the day. One of us would play on a small handheld gaming console, while the rest of us would watch. We spent most of our morning together. During lunch, we had the most crowded table in the cafeteria. The cafeteria workers always stuffed our lunches and a carton of milk or juice on a small, plastic tray that most people ate from in about ten minutes. When we were ready to leave, a teacher outside the cafeteria handed us pink passes (notes signed off by a teacher) that we needed to visit the library. Our usual hideout lay in the back left corner of the room. We didn't do much when we were there. Most of my time was spent talking and eating whatever leftovers I had in my lunchbox until the school bell rang. Due to our unique scheduling conflicts, we didn't have another class for about twenty minutes. Still, I left the library quickly and followed a crowd of students two floors up to the Writing Lab (a place for writing support), so I could use one of their computers for schoolwork before they were all occupied. The Writing Lab was a fun place. Its teaching staff was, at one point, able to recognize almost all of the visiting students by face and name. Small birthday celebrations were held here, and student literary work was hung throughout the room.

Most of the people in my group of friends recognized that I appreciated math the most. We had a Math Lab (place for math support) that we also visited right outside the school library. Usually, only one or two other kids were there working on their schoolwork or preparing their own little projects. When the room was quiet, a teacher who we would frequently interact with approached us. He already knew what we were here for and watched us play hangman on the whiteboard using nearby markers. It didn't take very long for us to draw the head, arms, and legs. But to be fair, we also couldn't forget the hat, shoes, nose, eyes, and face.

I was not big on meeting my friends after school. I never had a ride to get me places, and the only way I could get transportation home was through the school's late-bus program. All riders needed a pink pass from a teacher who could prove they stayed after school for school-related reasons, so I ended up joining the Math Team within the first month of the school year. It was held at the NFA Main Campus. As the name implies, it's the lead high school. Thankfully, the Math Team was not a club of nerds like everyone expected it to be. The teacher in charge bought granola bars, chips, and candy before each meeting and placed them on her classroom's front desk for the taking. She ran the program and taught Algebra for over a decade. Every year, she signed kids up to compete in math competitions in the county. Contrary to what you may expect, after school life was lively at Main. I hardly found myself in an empty hallway. You could always find laughter within classrooms and the school band preparing for their next performance. Sometimes when I was in the building, I'd see my middle school classmates and friends. The last time I said hello to some of them was four years earlier. At the end of my sixth-grade year, I transferred out to a different middle school for reasons beyond my control. One time when I was walking to an after school debate team meeting, a group of former classmates saw me from their classroom and all ran outside with excitement to greet me. I couldn't get in a word because they were so happy.

My life couldn't have been better. Every Tuesday around sundown, my dad was dressed in a blue-collared shirt and tan dress pants. He always received a quick kiss on the cheek from my mother before entering another school board meeting. I remember watching him take the oath of office in front of at least a hundred people before I started eighth grade (around 2014). As he placed his left hand on a Bible, he held his right hand up and repeated every word spoken to him. A historic number of people were interested in winning one of the Board of Education's four open seats, and my father was voted into the position after campaigning against thirteen other candidates. His victory was a big moment for Newburgh because the NECSD just hired a new Superintendent.

During my father's first few years in office, he was ecstatic. Prior to joining the BOE, his usual routine would be to work from 9 a.m. to 5 p.m. at the land surveying company that he founded. He had so much strength that he would hike through mountains and hills to create property deeds for homeowners, an excruciating task for even the most skilled land surveyors. On top of that, he would return home and hold my then six-month-old brother in his arms. He made dinner for my then twelve-year-old brother and I as we were watching the television, finishing homework, or playing video games. Unlike previous years, we would all make time to eat together at the dining room table or within our living room as we told one another about what our day was like. Local politics didn't matter to me until late in my freshman year of high school because I had a loving family. Around that time, I saw school custodians covering up the water fountains with plastic sheets. In a decision made the previous day, Newburgh's City Council declared a state of emergency after announcing Lake Washington - the city's water supply - was contaminated with PFOS.[1] It's a highly-toxic chemical used for fire suppression. Within two hours of school opening for the day, water bottles were delivered to the high schools. Kids were on the verge of passing out from dehydration.

While it might not have seemed like it at the high school, dehydration was one of the smaller issues Newburgh faced at that time. The actual water supply the students drank from at home was a much bigger concern. Imagine a mother mixing baby formula, or a pregnant woman pouring herself a glass of water. A local environmental organization indicated these simple acts in Newburgh may have put an entire generation of children at risk of someday developing cancer.[2] Parents and elders cooked with it, bathed themselves in it, and allowed their kids to brush their teeth with it. Overnight, this story attracted the attention of everyone in New York, so all of the newspapers and cable news companies ran similar front headlines: "Newburgh Declares State of Emergency."

Newburgh rarely has significant states of emergencies, and no one in my hometown ever thought they'd live through such an immense water problem. Much of the city had already heard about similar water crises in places like Flint, Michigan where the water looked and smelled foul. However, Newburgh's case was different. Our water supply looked perfectly normal, convincing a whole generation of people to believe there was nothing wrong. Things got so serious that the state government secured an alternative water supply from a neighboring community.[3] A lead figure of a local environmental organization told the media, "People are very concerned about their health, obviously. This has been in the drinking water supply for years. We may have exposed a whole generation to this contaminant!"[4] My school let me start a research project about PFOS. I felt like an expert after reading the reports for hours. I could cite everything about where the pollution came from or what the chemicals were made of. Newburgh's community did a lot to tackle the crisis. The State Department of Health offered free blood tests.[5] Community cleanups were held throughout the city. These efforts, along with many other initiatives, were part of an entire volunteering awareness crusade aimed at taking back our rivers and streets.

The water didn't smell funny, the color didn't look odd, and it was not unpleasant to consume, yet PFOS is strong enough to kill children fairly quickly. The school district was also affected by the water crisis. Not only did the NECSD have to confront PFOS, but they also had a lead problem. Out of all the fountains examined in the schools, 105 of their water fountains (about ten percent) "exceeded the acceptable level set by the federal government."[6] In a thirty-person classroom, around three people would leave the class every hour to drink from them. The district vowed to fix them, and they later did.

Around that time, my freshman year was ending. In preparation for the summer and the end of the school year, the BOE became very busy. My father recently began attending very tense school board meetings, where the stakes only got higher and higher each week. Normally the meetings ended around four hours before midnight. During this time, though, my father would sometimes come home an hour after midnight. He told me that the superintendent and other administrators gave them several more grants and other proposals to review. It would stretch the imagination to believe the explosion of grants and funds did not have to do with an upcoming contract extension vote for one of the lead administrators within the school district. I always heard something about the contract when I got home from school. If five board members did not vote to approve the upcoming contract, the district official would have to leave in 2017. There was apparently a concern among the official's supporters that he wouldn't get the five votes.

One morning, an article appeared in the front headlines of Newburgh's most popular newspaper. What my father found astounding when reading this article over bacon and toast was how half of the report spread "rumors" about four board members, whose identities were all published, because they "may resist an extension."[7] One of the names was my dad's. The author's source came from a petition made by an anonymous person online who claimed to be a "Newburgh Free Academy Educator," but the reporter never says he verified their identity.[8] He was also given a statement by the BOE's attorney which said my father had been advised of the board's practice "not to make public statements regarding matters of personnel decision making."[9] If a board member commented on whether or not they would fire someone prior to the vote, the employee in question might be able to use that statement against the NECSD in litigation.

Once I heard about the article, I wasn't concerned about anything pertaining to the administrator. This had little to do with him. I was more worried about my dad's safety. Days earlier, my mother and one of my brothers told me about two carloads of men who drove back and forth by my house after school while my dad and I were inside.[10] My then twelve-year-old brother was playing with a hockey stick in the driveway. The men watched them closely, monitoring their each and every action. Almost as if begging for their attention, one of the men stuck his arm out of the window from time to time. Another would shout our home address. We didn't know any of them, and we weren't expecting guests. By the time my dad called the police and an officer arrived on the scene, the men were long gone. The best we could do was file a police report.[11] For the remainder of the school year, the police planned to show up at our house immediately if any of us called them.

The administrator in question was in a powerful enough position to tackle city-wide issues from an educational perspective. Given the anxiety that much of my hometown had at the time, Newburgh needed a strong leader. Some people felt like he was qualified, while the BOE may have had reason to believe otherwise. The stakes were all the more reason for my family to be concerned about my father's well-being. Halfway through his article, the reporter wrote when and where the next board meeting would take place. Although the contract extension vote wouldn't be held until the following week, my family recognized that my dad may be confronted by an angry group of people. They all had the option of not showing their faces at the meeting. Amazingly, my father and the others chose to stand up for themselves. Desperate times called for desperate measures. During his spare time, I saw my dad finalize a plan of what to do if he was confronted by an angry group. This planning was necessary because the City of Newburgh isn't known for being a safe place at night. When my father was about to leave, I hugged him in the living room before he left. My entire family gathered in a circle, with all our prayers directed at his safety.

News of the article garnished so many headlines that the BOE had to relocate its meeting to another school, which can hold hundreds more people. He walked into one of the most crowded meeting rooms he's ever attended. Normally, this place is used for student performances. It has a massive stage to the right of the entrance. Chairs for spectators were laid out facing the stage and a series of desks reserved for the eight board members, the superintendent, the Board Clerk, and other district officials. A few minutes past seven, the talking died down. As the NECSD's BOE President spoke using a microphone, someone started recording the meeting in the background.[12] The meeting was going to be divided based on what the BOE originally planned to discuss (agenda items) and additional concerns that the local residents had about the school system (non-agenda items).

"We have no one signed up for [discussing board] agenda items at this time. Is there anyone in the audience who would like to address the audience on agenda items?"[13]

A woman clothed in black tentatively stood up. Everyone was quiet and attentive, wondering what she was going to say or do. The President gestured for her to approach a brown podium with a microphone at the front of the room.

"Please state your name and the agenda item that you're speaking of."

"I am here to speak on the agenda item in reference to the vote that's going to be taken regarding the administrator-"

"I'm sorry," the President interrupted. "That's not on-"

"That's not on the agenda this evening?" the woman insisted.

"No."

"Really? Woah!" Everyone behind her laughed. "Wait! Wait! You're telling me that's not on the agenda, but we're seeing it in newspapers and everything. This is a top issue. It's not on the agenda?"

"If you look at the agenda, no it's not on the agenda."

"Well, when will it be and when will people be able to speak on it?"

"When we prepare the next agenda."

"So it's not going to be handled in this meeting?" she asked a fourth time.

"Not in this meeting."

"So is the vote going to be taken this evening?"

You could start to hear the groans. Same question, same answer.

"This is not a question and answer session," the President responded.

"Well, I would like to know! Is the vote going to be taken regarding this issue or not this evening?"

"I can't give you that."

"You can't give me that?"

"No."

"Ok. You will hear my answer. Thank you."

It was not clear what she meant by her "answer," but the woman finished on a mountain of praise. The photographer near the stage got excited and started taking pictures of the audience murmuring as the woman returned to her seat. A few people at the front of the room exchanged glances; others gave off confused looks.

"Would anyone else like to address the Board on agenda items only?"

The room was silent. No one replied.

"Thank you. We'll move on. First reading of policy number 5000: student policy goals."

The BOE proceeded pretty quickly with its policy components and committee reports. Unlike other meetings, this one consisted of celebrations where students and teachers were awarded certificates of honor for their strong dedication to an academic subject. The meeting highlighted the winner of an essay contest who wrote about a civil rights figure who influenced them, the top performing Math Team students from each elementary school, and a physical education teacher who was honored by the New York State Alliance for Health, Physical Education, Recreation, and Dance. Proceeding through the BOE's agenda items lasted thirty minutes.

"We're now at the public discussion of non-agenda items," said the Board President.

One of the board members interrupted the speech by addressing the President directly. "Yes?" she responded.[14]

"Yes, Madame President. I would like to move that we extend this portion of the meeting in light of the fact that we talked about agenda items for thirty minutes. But more importantly, we have a large room of students, stakeholders, parents, teachers, and former students in the audience who have come out tonight and have the right to be heard. I think that it would be unfair to them if we [don't] allow their voices to be heard. We are in the middle of some very important conversations that will be had and will be significantly impacting the children of our district, in addition to their future. We don't want it to be said that we did not give the public a chance to be heard. Madame President, I would like to extend the thirty-minute rule [used to limit the total time spent on hearing from the public], but ask that we keep intact the five-minute per speaker rule."

"How long would you like to extend it for?"

"Well, we had a short meeting tonight. I would like to hear from anyone that likes to be heard."

That last sentence created one of the loudest rounds of applause of the night.

"Let's put a time limit on it. We do have another executive session [a session for the BOE to discuss confidential information]. So, do you want it to be forty-five minutes? An hour?"

"Ninety minutes."

"Ninety!"

It's not routine for the BOE to extend the time they hear from its constituents by an hour. In light of the attention that the other news story received, having the public speak for ninety minutes could generate more press.

"I would like to obtain a motion please,"[15] the President followed up. A few seconds passed.

"Any questions for discussion?" No one answered.

"Roll call, Mr. Clerk."

One by one, the Clerk called the names of each board member. There was unanimous consensus, including those who might not support the administrator. No one on the BOE could really object to transparent government.

"Ok!" the President started reading off her tablet. "We are now at the public participation [session], which is limited to five minutes per speaker for a total of ninety minutes for all speakers. There is a timer in front of the room that will keep track of your time. The timer will begin when you start to address the Board. Please direct your comments to the entire Board and not to individual members. If you have any questions regarding a public comment, please refer to the public comment procedure form that is available by the sign-in sheet. Public participation is not a question and answer session for the Board. If you would like an answer to your question, please submit your request in writing to the Board Clerk."

She looked ahead at the woman dressed in black as she approached the podium to speak again.

"Um... We have a list of signed up people [to speak], and you're on it. So, can we call them first, please?"

"Yes, you may." She would have to give her "answer" later.

There was already so much concern about emotions running high that night. While none of the speakers mentioned the water crisis, the talk of the town for the past two months had been about the children. "The children" was the buzzword of nearly every speech. Despite how his supporters attended this meeting, one individual claimed the administrator had been "rejected" like the children and that this official could help these kids. She expressed her sadness in the form of a song. After finishing her song, she gave a speech.[16]

> *"What about the children?"*
> *"To ignore [them] is so easy."*
> *"So many innocent children!"*
> *"Who choose the wrong way."*
> *"What about the children?"*
> *"Remember when we were children."*
> *And if it not for those who loved us."*
> *"And to carry love to show us."*
> *"Where would we be today?"*

"What would we be today, if there wasn't somebody who helped you through this struggle?" she asked the audience. "Where would you be? I worked at South [Junior] High (a local middle school) as a substitute, and I love South High because those children are so rejected because of the reputation [the school] has been given. And I hear from the teachers, 'Oh, we can't do anything. We can't suspend them.' Don't suspend them. Love them! Love our children! That's what they need! They need love! That's what this city needs is love! Do you have it in you to love! Love will cure! Toss it to them! Start loving people! Start loving the children! These children..."

Soon, more people stood up and spoke specifically about the board members. A former elected representative in Newburgh portrayed the BOE members as people who need to "put aside personal agendas [and] put away power struggles."[17] Another former official also spoke against the alleged critics. "Most of you sit here because the union has sought you out and has endorsed you. I do believe in unions. However, I don't believe in bullying, nepotism, personal agendas, or vendettas."[18] Although she did not win re-election, the individual alleged they continued to "manipulate" and "micromanage" this district. "I think if you're giving everyone mentors, you should seriously consider getting mentors for yourselves as a board!"[19] For nearly ninety minutes, the four board members heard the public's various opinions and thoughts. Toward the end of the meeting, the woman clothed in black finally gave her "answer." She said, "I'm making a promise. I'm making a promise that if you do not do the right thing, *you're going to live to regret it*. Because I got people ready to come into the City of Newburgh because they are concerned about our children."[20]

My father later told me that he was concerned about these comments as a few more speakers stepped forward. Before anyone realized it, the ninety minutes were up. The President then interjected at the very end.

"Thank you! I'm sorry, but we have really taken up our ninety minutes. We have to continue because we have executive session now, so thank you very much for all of your comments. Be it resolved that the Board of Education hereby recesses into executive session for the following purpose: matters made confidential under FERPA [Family Educational Rights and Privacy Act], employment history of particular individuals, matters linked to the employment of particular individuals, the review and placement of programs for students with disabilities, and collective bargaining. I'd like to obtain a motion please."

An hour after the BOE went into executive session for private discussions, my dad came home.

"You're back!" my mom exclaimed.

My father had so much news to share. The meeting was recorded, and a video of its contents was posted on the Internet. I saw everything my dad witnessed the next day, including the public discussion on agenda items, the apparent threats, and even the individual singing. Watching it was disturbing in some instances, though it was amusing in others.

"These are them." My mom paused the video after a group of men turned around to leave the podium. She believed these were the individuals who drove by our house.

My brother agreed. He has a photographic memory for faces. When he looks at someone, he knows immediately whether he has seen them before. Some of the people who the men were with stated their name for the meeting record, allowing my dad to call the police precinct with this information. Unfortunately, we were out of luck. They said they needed the name of the specific individual who pointed at my house and shouted my address to start an investigation.

Around the weekend before the vote, my dad received a call from a friend of his on the BOE. Certain people allegedly had made this past week so stressful for my father's friend that he was now urging my father to vote alongside him in favor of the administrator. Years following this incident, I posted something on social media about a completely different issue within the district. Even though I don't know this BOE member personally, he oddly responded back by discussing this meeting. He revealed that he "express[ed] his concerns to some members of the Board and was advised to remain quiet because they did not want any consequences/trouble in the community."[21] As soon as I read that, I remembered what my father told me about what the BOE member was going through shortly after the recorded meeting. I couldn't believe that hurtful rhetoric could really influence the way people voted.

One week later, my father left the household with even more prayers from my family. This would be the meeting where the contract extension vote was being held. It was recorded in the NFA Main auditorium. Similar to the last meeting, the BOE President was the first individual to use her microphone.

"Good evening everyone!"[22] the Board President announced at the start of the meeting. The room hushed itself down.

"We're going to change around the [Board] protocol here. So, the first thing I would like to do is read this resolution and then we're going to do the scholar athlete awards."

She began with the spectators clapping at the news about the change in plans. In a unanimous vote taken earlier within the hour, the President announced that the BOE extended the contract.

Within seconds, the one-hundred-person audience gave the administrator a standing ovation along with the rest of the BOE. With his hands crossed over his suit, he walked over to the first four board members who weren't criticized in the newspaper and hugged them. Then, he relaxed his posture and hugged the remaining board members on his left. When he returned back to his seat, the cheering died down, though one person in the background decided to shout a short remark.

"Can I have a motion please?" the Board President asked. A few seconds passed.

"Questions for discussion?"

"Roll call, Mr. Clerk."

It is amazing how one local news article could influence the history of its town. One week after publishing a story about rumors which claimed four board members were against the extension, the press revealed that the BOE somehow unanimously approved it. From what the evidence shows, stress influenced the BOE's decision. I understand the official may not have been involved, but this situation taught me about what creates bad politics. While there were many parents who had heartfelt personal reasons to support the administrator, I'm not disputing the good that he may have brought to Newburgh. For example, one former teacher noted during the first BOE meeting that the administrator gave up an entire Sunday just to watch him get inducted into the National Wrestling Hall of Fame. This has nothing to do with him. I'm also not concerned about whether the rumor was true. This was about how certain people damaged my father's integrity over an opinion.

My freshman year served as a crash course into politics. Dad's experiences as a school board member introduced it in the household, and the town's environmental crisis introduced it in the schools. Consequently, I became fascinated with the issues shaping Newburgh at a very young age. After this incident, board politics became relevant to my life on a daily basis. I do try to get along with those whose ideas and beliefs don't align with my own. Regardless of what happened to my family, I do look at all of the facts first. The people at NFA North are very kind and caring. Newburgh is truly a good community with good people who want to move forward. Unfortunately, my hometown still had a long way to go. The BOE member who commented on one of my earlier social media posts also stated, "I don't understand how we can expect our children\ students to do the right thing when the people in charge are leading by such a poor example. Leading by fear, intimidation, bullying to name a few have no place in our lives but especially not in education. Staff, faculty, students, and even parents should never feel that they can't speak up without retaliation. Unfortunately it has been going on too long in the NECSD. The NECSD is in just as much turmoil and distress as our nation."[23] So this book isn't just about some small town in the northeast. What happens in Newburgh is reflective of our nation's political climate. This story is what got my interest in politics to begin with because it was a call to action. In response to my book, the same BOE member added, "Thank you, Mr. Stridiron, for leading by such a courageous example of what it looks like when we are doing the right thing."[24]

CHAPTER ENDNOTES

1   Checkey Beckford, "Newburgh Declares State of Emergency After Chemical Found in Drinking Water," May 3, 2016, https://www.nbcnewyork.com/news/local/newburgh-state-of-emergency-water-chemical-pfos/728882/

2   "Contamination of the Drinking Water Reservoir and Watershed of the City of Newburgh: A Case Study And A Call For Comprehensive Source Water Protection," *Newburgh: Riverkeeper*, 2016. https://www.riverkeeper.org/wp-content/uploads/2016/08/White-Paper-Newburgh- Source-Water-Protection-FINAL-2.pdf

3   Leonard Sparks, "Newburgh's use of Brown's Pond for water raises concerns in New Windsor," *Times Herald-Record*, May 4, 2016, https://www.recordonline.com/story/news/2016/05/04/newburgh-s-use-brown-s/30920929007/

4   "Nine months later, PFOS pollution from the Stewart Air National Guard Base continues unabated," *Riverkeeper*, January 5, 2017, https://www.riverkeeper.org/blogs/docket/nine-months-later-pfos-pollution-stewart-air-national-guard-base-continues-unabated/

5   New York Department of Health, "New York State Department of Health Announces Free Newburgh Blood Testing Program for PFOS Exposure Extended through December 31" news release, October 16, 2017, https://www.health.ny.gov/press/releases/2017/2017-10-06_newburgh_blood_testing_extension.htm

6   Paul Brooks, "Newburgh schools dealing with high lead levels in water," *Times Herald-Record*, May 5, 2016, https://www.recordonline.com/story/news/2016/05/05/newburgh-schools-dealing-with-high/30883890007/

7   Leonard Sparks, "Supporters seek extension for Newburgh school superintendent," *Times Herald-Record*, June 10, 2016, https://www.recordonline.com/story/news/education/2016/06/10/supporters-seek-extension-for-newburgh/27956791007/

8   Newburgh Free Academy Educator, "NECSD Students, Educators, Parents, and Community Members in Support of Dr. Padilla," https://www.change.org/p/silent-rally-this-tuesday-in-support-of-dr-padilla

9   Sparks, "Supporters seek extension for Newburgh school superintendent."

10   See deposition in Google Drive (pages 104-112)

11   Police report can be found in Google Drive.

12   Newburgh Teachers Association, "Newburgh ECSD BOE Meeting 6/14/2016," June 16, 2016, Youtube video, 2:23:41, https://www.youtube.com/watch?v=7xuSsgpaeLk

13   Newburgh Teachers Association, "Newburgh ECSD BOE Meeting 6/14/2016," clip starts at 47:00

14   Newburgh Teachers Association, "Newburgh ECSD BOE Meeting 6/14/2016," clip starts at 48:30

15   Ibid, clip starts at 48:30

16   Ibid, clip starts at 2:09:00

17   Ibid, clip starts at 1:40:00

18   Ibid, clip starts at 1:02:30

19   Ibid

20   Ibid, clip starts at 1:56:00

21   Social media post. See https://www.facebook.com/matthew.stridiron.5/posts/447576309564336

22   Newburgh Teachers Association, "Newburgh ECSD BOE Meeting 6/21/2016," June 21, 2016, Youtube video, 1:29:37, https://www.youtube.com/watch?v=LyXoXifY6vE, see beginning of clip

23   Social media post. See https://www.facebook.com/matthew.stridiron.5/posts/447576309564336

24   Social media post. See https://www.facebook.com/matthew.stridiron.5/posts/447576309564336

3
CHILDREN CAUGHT IN THE MIDDLE
2011 – 2016

During the fall of my junior year, one of my younger brothers wanted me to join him on the school's Mock Trial team. Like much of my family, my brother loved watching crime shows and got to see everything that unravels in a courtroom. Attorneys preparing for an actual trial might use a mock trial consisting of volunteers as role players to test theories on how certain witnesses will react to their specific questions. My brother's team needed someone to write up questions for a case he would be a star witness for. The fictional case investigated how a school district's administrators retaliated against children. Supposedly, each building administrator worked in a coordinated attempt with their school's resource officers to arrest students struggling in classes days before they were supposed to sit for a district-wide assessment. These tests affected taxpayer satisfaction with the school district. If students performed poorly, the town wouldn't fund the schools. By removing a large percentage of these kids from the school a week before the exam date for several years in a row, the administrators artificially boosted the test scores. My biggest task focused on developing questions surrounding these points, particularly the actual motive behind the grade manipulation and how this case affected future students. I felt like it was a good role for me because I was much more interested in public education at the time.

Overcoming my sophomore year in high school was no easy task. Although my grades were high, they didn't reflect what I was going through at home. Every weekend, the BOE would release an agenda to the public describing what they would be discussing at the next meeting. This notice gave the BOE members around four days to prepare. People like the BOE member who wrote on social media, to my knowledge, always had immense support at these meetings, yet they were oftentimes the individuals who got the most pushback. Yet as the BOE member said, he neither has an agenda nor intends to make anyone look bad. Instead, he and others are doing what they see as in the best interest of students. There are many great people like that board member, though most of them don't say anything out of concern of this very pushback. However, as part of this book, one of NFA's teachers was willing to talk with me about how the state of education has changed over the course of her nearly thirty-year career for four hours. Her views are her own, and we agreed that she would remain anonymous throughout the entirety of *Scheming In the Dark*. I neither intend to release her name nor specify whether she is retired. She did not come to me as a whistleblower, yet rather as someone who wants to see things change for the better. Since taking on the role of a teacher, she has watched the NECSD transform under the leadership of five different superintendents and has spoken at several BOE meetings. She told me her lengthy time at the NECSD makes her a valuable speaker for issues at the BOE in the eyes of her peers.

During an exceptional year like 2010, sports dominated the local news. The teacher I talked to frequently attended football games with her children at NFA. More impressively, the NECSD's basketball team won ninety percent of the games in their season. They were led by the "Super Six," the top six performing seniors who alone brought Newburgh to the state championship finals. One of the Super Six members was hailed as the Basketball Player of the Year by Newburgh's lead newspaper.[1] The basketball team won the state championships in 2009 against the Niagara Falls City School District, putting the players on their dream routes straight to college basketball. NFA's Player of the Year wanted to play in college and was offered a full scholarship for his athletic abilities.[2] With that kind of name recognition circulating the state, these players had what very few high school graduates could ever hope to achieve in four years. In another article, one of the basketball players told the press that he wanted to either pursue a career in the National Basketball Association (NBA) or overseas as a businessman.[3]

Just one year after the Super Six graduated, a sports journalist from Newburgh's lead newspaper interviewed them. He wanted to know whether they were on track to reaching their career goals. What they told him amazed his team. While many in the sports realm praised their exceptional talent, the athletes themselves told a different story. The six players now spent their days playing basketball outside a local church and gym, two of them attended prep school for college, and just one was enrolled at a university.[4,5] Most of them didn't graduate. Their big achievements were in the past, so they constantly reflected on what they used to be like in high school. This regression caused their closest friends to give up on them, and it ate at their confidence every time they thought about it. For example, the reporter learned that the same Super Six member who wanted to go overseas still had newspapers about family, basketball players, and Newburgh winning the state title hanging on his bedroom walls.[6] He looked up to LeBron James because he said Lebron is "living the life and playing the game he loves."[7] The stress of not being on track to reach his dreams and become someone like Lebron James was unbearable. He suffered from a nervous breakdown and was diagnosed with psychosis, a loss of contact with reality, before eventually having to take prescription drugs.[8] In his own words, it's tough to be a state champion when he fails. "If we lose, everybody looks at us and says, 'What happened?' But people like to watch us play because, I guess, we're fun to watch."[9]

Landing free throws and slam dunks is something the Super Six dreamed of since they were very young. The teacher I talked with recalled from her experiences with them, "They were great friends and had lots of on-court chemistry. Most of my interaction with them would have been in a cafeteria or on another supervisory duty that we are assigned at school. I often found them to be inordinately polite. 'Hello, Mrs.' 'How are you doing today, Mrs?' That kind of stuff. Even though they didn't have a class with me, they were polite kids. They would often have a pink pass signed by an administrator that would allow them in the lunchroom, even if it wasn't their lunch period." (She clarified that pink passes are legal excuses signed off by an administrator that allow students to be anywhere in the high school.)

Despite how the basketball players were good kids who had excused absences, she wasn't too surprised when she first heard they didn't graduate. "I didn't think they were learning much in the classes they were in because they always had a pink pass to be somewhere else." She would see them very often. If they rarely go to class, one would expect for them to have bad grades. (According to her, the NECSD has a four-quarter academic system. The first semester incorporates the first and second quarters. The second semester incorporates the third and fourth quarters. Averaging the grades of each quarter, you need at least 65 on a 100-point scale to pass.) However, one of the athletes recalled, "I didn't even really go to [science] class after the first quarter (first ten weeks of school), and I never got over a 65 on a test. I ended up with an 80."[10] With a decent GPA, his family didn't understand why he couldn't graduate. How can you not graduate if you earn high grades? And how can you earn high grades if you're always in the cafeteria?

For people like the sports journalist, the answer to these questions is what made this situation analogous to a mystery. Normally when students have an excessive number of absences on their record, most people would expect a teacher or administrator to contact the parents about the cuts. It turns out, though, that the attendance records of these basketball players did not even come close to accurately reflecting the severity of their situation. According to documents obtained by the reporter as part of his investigation, the Super Six accumulated a total of 1187 cuts within just one school year. Of these cuts, 649 of them were excused."[11] These changes likely prevented the players from getting the educational support they needed.

It's hard to believe that student athletes themselves would just admit to participating in such a system, yet the teachers have seen their previous students land in this same situation over and over again. The teacher I interviewed told me that her colleagues were aware of the mysterious changes, and they were not the ones who excused the cuts. According to the interview, the Newburgh Teachers Association (NTA) intervened by calling special meetings to inform NFA's faculty about the attendance problems. The instructor told me, "You could see how easy it was for students to be somewhere else in the building, even though we didn't have an open school campus. You could see how easy it was for students to be somewhere else in the building rather than in class."

All of these revelations amazed the sports journalist who interviewed the basketball players. For his job, he was writing about a very intriguing story. How and why were hundreds of absences excused in front of teachers who never even authorized the change? He wanted to know more. Rumors floated throughout the city as to who or what may have been responsible. People like the teacher who I interviewed argue that the mysterious changes are part of a much larger problem in poor communities across the country. There is a large population of students who are already discouraged from going to school, but in most states, having a clean attendance record guarantees graduation as long as a student has a high enough GPA (such as the 80 in the science class). Although they can get a diploma, they are not prepared for much beyond high school. From her experiences, having an excessive number of unprepared students can create many local problems for three reasons: 1) the excessive skipping affects graduates to the point where they can't find a job, 2) they are stuck on the streets, and 3) ignoring the problem can cause it to span decades. Think of all the graduates like the Super Six throughout the country who may have been left jobless, homeless, and without a college education after leaving high school. Many people are still without a college education in the City of Newburgh today. While the people who skipped classes do bear some of the blame for where they ended up, they could have been saved had they received the right support. It is easy to understand why this is such an important topic for someone who's worked in education for nearly three decades.

Newburgh's former Player of the Year told the sports reporter, "It's tough missing something I love to do. It's frustrating, I really want to get into college. A lot of people might have given up on me, but I want to prove them wrong."[12] Their stories surprised the journalist, and he made it his mission to have the whole community know what was going on. He wrote up a lengthy two-day special report that his newspaper put on its front cover. It was so popular that he was even called into interviews that were later posted on Youtube. "I don't think, for the most part, anything like what's going on in Newburgh is going on anywhere else," he said. "This story started as a simple 'Where are they now?' kind of story. So many of the kids hadn't graduated, and I wanted to talk to them about that.[13]

Despite how the story started out as a local report, it became extremely popular within days of reaching the front page of the newspaper. News of the Super Six made regional headlines and even reached Niagara Falls.[14] While other people who lived outside Newburgh were shocked by the news, local graduates didn't appear very surprised. A 1984 NFA graduate said this class cutting doesn't date back just five or six years. It dates back three decades. "They win a state championship, and the kids are left on the streets. As long as you play basketball [...], you are going to be alright. You don't have to go to classes. It was like that when I played. When does it stop?"[15] There was enough unease in the region to attract the attention of the National Association for the Advancement of Colored People (NAACP), who announced they would conduct their own investigation alongside the district. Given their international reputation, their involvement was a pretty big deal. "Silence is always a concern," the President of the local NAACP responded. "In this case, it's a critical concern. It's not easy to defend silence. I'm sure it won't continue; it can't. Ultimately, they (the district) have to come out and say something about this debacle."[16]

Watching my hometown come together during this very difficult time is a testament to the strength of a community which really wanted answers. Starting in May 2011, an aspiring board member began uploading footage of the board meetings and other community events onto Youtube. There was immense interest in the May 2011 BOE meeting because the NECSD announced they began interviewing the athletes and around fifty other employees in question.[17] Newburgh's NAACP also held monthly meetings in the City of Newburgh, one of which was recorded by the same aspiring board member. It was held late at night, but all of the chairs were filled. All attendees were introduced to the organization's regional director before he explained the findings of their investigation with the NECSD. "We initially came here involving the incident that occurred. However, we quickly realized that the magnitude of this problem is much greater than any one incident."[18] He asked the NECSD for several statistics in May 2011 to learn who was most affected. The NAACP wanted the number of students who graduated, were suspended, performed above and below their grade level, attended two or four-year institutions, and entered the workforce. An NFA North Assistant Principal (AP) who also worked in the district for thirty years like the teacher I interviewed praised the NAACP for their efforts at this event.[19] "Some of us have been fighting the fight for a while, and we will continue to fight. But we do get weary, and we need a lot of help. But the fact of the matter is, we do it because of these children." He stated, "We all stand to gain if everyones' needs are addressed."

The AP's presence at the NAACP meeting signified that the 2011 basketball attendance problems was not a community vs. district administration kind of struggle. Just as the board member in the previous chapter showed, people across all levels of the district agreed that the community needed some form of remedy to this situation so kids could thrive. At one point, even the BOE's attorney acknowledged "systematic failures" following an off-camera meeting with the NAACP.[20] He sought to answer the following question with the help of a forensic auditor: "Were the members of the 2008-2009 and 2009-2010 boys basketball team allowed to cut classes?"[21] He explained that all reasons for excusing an absence are each given their own attendance code, which is a computerized ID that specifies the reason. However, the Commissioner of Education (the top person who runs the NYSED) required the district to develop what's called a "Comprehensive Student Attendance Policy" in 2002. This specific legislation contains "very strict exceptions for excused absences," rendering most of the original attendance codes useless. Still, those codes were never removed from the NECSD's attendance system. When the NECSD bought a new attendance system, those invalid codes were still used. The BOE's attorney admitted, "The use of other excused absences, in the case of student-athletes and other students, in the attendance codes was in violation of board policy and has been for over eight years."

The attorney's admission ended the debate of whether there were massive attendance problems. "Upon learning of this systemic failure and the operation of the attendance system," the attorney continued, "the Board of Education sought answers to these questions. How could this have happened? Was there malfeasance or only nonfeasance? Should there be accountability in the form of disciplinary proceedings? Our investigation revealed that when the new attendance policy was implemented in 2002, there was a lack of administrative oversight that resulted in the continual use of the other excused absence codes in the student attendance system."[22] In the event that someone was responsible for the changes as opposed to it being solely a machine error, he vowed that "[t]o the extent that there exists reliable evidence of neglect of duty and or conduct unbecoming professional staff members, it has been and remains the Board's policy to address the same through due process pre-disciplinary proceedings."

At the November 2011 board meeting, though, the BOE's attorney gave a heartbreaking, unceremonious announcement for many in the room.[23] Halfway into the meeting, the superintendent (a different superintendent from the one hired in 2014) allowed the BOE's attorney to provide insight into the NECSD's "final report" on the attendance problems. It uncovered no names and revealed no disciplinary measures. A majority of its content was never even released to the public to my knowledge, except for the part that the attorney read. Despite interviewing fifty-seven district employees, his investigation "did not produce further significant evidence" of misconduct that "implicated staff members in a manner for which disciplinary action should follow."[24]

The room was filled with a dull silence when he finished speaking.[25] Public speakers gave their prepared statements for another hour, to which everyone also eyed closely, but only one teacher responded to the attorney's statement. Although the BOE indicated they would not look into this matter any further, the psychological and academic impacts on the kids did not go unnoticed. After the news coverage created by the final report, the teacher I spoke with remembers that other teachers weren't happy. She said many of the students earn scholarships that require them to accrue a certain number of college credits. Since they frequently missed school, they did not learn what they needed to in high school and had to take remedial (developmental) courses at college. These remedial courses did not count as college credit, which overwhelmed their academic workload. Soon, many of them lost their scholarships, couldn't pay for school, and returned back to the streets of Newburgh within a matter of years.

Of the graduates who enrolled in developmental English at college, a vast majority of them struggled. During the most shocking part of the interview, the teacher said her goal has always been to improve student reading comprehension. She noted that "We had a whole generation of adolescent teenagers who really couldn't read. They guessed, based on the signature of letters, what words were." Take "abducted" as an example of such a word. On a sheet of loose-leaf paper, the halfway point between any of its two lines is called the "median." B's, d's, t's, and f's go above the median. P's, q's, and g's extend below the median in lower case. "They might know what a 'b' looks like, but in a word, they might assume a 'd' was a 'b!' They hadn't learned letters and the sounds that letters make through phonics. If you gave them just the letter, they would be able to tell you what the letter was. But when it was in a word like 'abducted.' You have a 'b,' and a 'd,' and later you have a 't' and another 'd' that all extend above the median." When they saw the word "abducted" on a piece of paper, "they might not recognize it until you said what the word was." They thought the word was "aducted" instead of "abducted," or "any other version of how some of those letters looked [relative] to each other." The students she referred to neither had dysgraphia, dyslexia, nor any other sight impairments. They're considered "normal" high school students. We talked about other kinds of words they could mess up. "They just constantly guessed what a word was based on its kind of signature of letters that go above and below [the median]. They could easily mix up an 'm' and an 'n.' They could easily mess up a 'p' or a 'g.' B's and D's. T's and F's." This problem existed all over the community.

At a separate NAACP forum held in Newburgh, a former New Jersey administrator advised her supporters that parents would have to take matters into their own hands by being the "Frederick Douglasses of [their] district."[26] Frederick Douglass, for those who don't know, was an American abolitionist who fled from his slavemaster and ultimately became a pivotal figure in the fight to end slavery. The analogy that the New Jersey administrator used suggested Newburgh's youth are kept in a cycle of poverty against their will as a result of the decades-old class cutting problems, and the few individuals who manage to escape that cycle need to free their people from the same problem. "If you don't like what your school board is doing, then it's up to you to change it," the NAACP director added. "You need to organize. You should be registering everybody that you can possibly find to vote." As a source of inspiration, he stated, "There's a group in Rockland (a nearby county) that took over one of the districts in Rockland. They all got together. They all said they were gonna vote one way. They got 10,000 people, and they all went to the polls and voted."[27]

Cries to remove the board members were shouted over and over again by local residents at the NAACP forum. Public election records from 2011 and 2012 indicate that voters immediately responded to the 2011 class attendance problems.[28] Three or four people are appointed to the BOE each year. In both elections, two incumbents ran for office. One of them would keep their position in each election, while the other would lose it to a newcomer. The community was slow to respond at first. However, they ultimately replaced the BOE members. It took several years for them to be voted out because they serve three-year terms. By 2014, six of the nine sitting board members from 2011 were out of office.[29] Three incumbents happened to be running that year, and they were all defeated by people like my father.

Newburgh's community understands that getting to the bottom of what we can do to make children successful is a very important job. Changing public education so that students do not end up on the streets may also take some time, but it is good work that has profound consequences if you are patient enough. One of the reasons why the teacher spoke with me was because she understands places like Newburgh can be better. "We have this population that doesn't buy into the idea that [you] will make certain sacrifices or certain investments for a future payoff. And when you grow up in a cycle of poverty, there's no future payoff. And so as educators, many of us come from backgrounds where we have this belief and understanding of this idea of a current investment for a future payoff. We're trying to reach kids who don't rationalize and, in many ways, think about life in the way that we do because we are not ingrained in that cycle of poverty. The kids who don't go to school because it was pouring rain, or it snowed three days ago and half the people in the city don't shovel their sidewalks. They don't have anywhere safe to walk that's free from ice. They don't get that they are more likely to be stuck in that cycle of poverty because they don't go to school. They're not gonna graduate, or they're not gonna graduate on time. They're not gonna go to college, or they're not gonna finish college." Knowing this, I researched the biographies of some of the Super Six players to see how they're doing today. After doing an immense amount of research, I discovered that the Player of the Year eventually graduated.[30] However, I don't know what happened to the other Super Six members. None of the players whose contact information I was able to find responded to my request for comment. Most of the players don't come up on a Google search aside from the newspaper articles that are now over a decade old, which suggests that their lives have been damaged to the point where they could not reach their original career aspirations. The class cutting issues may also put students in a situation where they are stuck in a cycle of poverty after graduating. Reasons like these are what make school board politics so important. The people who spoke up in this chapter neither have an agenda nor intend to hurt the school system. Rather, they came with the best interest of the students in mind.

CHAPTER ENDNOTES

1   Kevin Witt, "V845 boys' basketball player of year: McLeod knows what it takes to win," *Times Herald-Record* April 11, 2010, https://www.recordonline.com/article/20100411/sports31/4110336

2   Kevin Witt, "Boys' basketball: Hello there, Newburgh guard Damon Cousar," *Times Herald-Record*, January 29, 2010, https://www.recordonline.com/article/20100129/SPORTS31/1290362

3   Ibid

4   Justin Rodriguez, "Part 2: Outside the lines, NFA's hoops heroes faltering," *Times Herald-Record*, March 7, 2011, https://www.recordonline.com/article/20110307/News/103070336

5   Justin Rodriguez, "NFA state hoops champs no-shows in classroom," *Times Herald-Record*, March 6, 2011, https://www.recordonline.com/article/20110306/News/103060321

6   Witt., "Boys' basketball: Hello there, Newburgh guard Damon Cousar."

7   Ibid

8   Rodriguez, "Part 2: Outside the lines, NFA's hoops heroes faltering."

9   Witt., "Boys' basketball: Hello there, Newburgh guard Damon Cousar."

10 Rodriguez, "NFA state hoops champs no-shows in classroom."

11 Justin Rodriguez, "NFA's records support players' claims about cuts," Times Herald-Record, April 11, 2011, https://www.recordonline.com/article/20110411/NEWS/104110320

12 Rodriguez, "Part 2: Outside the lines, NFA's hoops heroes faltering."

13 recordonline.com, "NFA Basketball Investigation," March 17, 2011, Youtube video, 2:52, https://www.youtube.com/watch?v=kSomVmxVuPA

14 "NFA class-cutting scandal timeline," *Times Herald-Record*, November 29, 2011, https://www.recordonline.com/article/20111129/sports/111290351

15 John Moriello, "Newburgh takes its lumps on and off court," New York State Sportswriters Association, March 9, 2011, http://www.newyorksportswriters.org/blog/2011-03-09-basketball-newburgh-free-academy.shtml

16 Justin Rodriguez, "NFA officials still silent about class-cutting scandal," *Times Herald-Record*, April 18, 2011, https://www.recordonline.com/article/20110418/news/104180334

17 newburghedinfo, "NECSD BOE 5-31-2011 1 of 4," June 3, 2011, Youtube video, 8:03, https://www.youtube.com/watch?v=7R-9fRFRhoiU

18 newburghedinfo, "NAACP 11-03-11," November 6, 2011, Youtube video, 1:20:16, https://www.youtube.com/watch?v=uFEJwFh-VtRQ, clip starts around 1:30

19 Ibid, clip starts around 52:50

20 Justin Rodriguez, "Newburgh district may take disciplinary steps in class-cutting scandal," *Times Herald-Record*, June 22, 2011. https://www.recordonline.com/story/news/2011/06/22/newburgh-district-may-take-disciplinary/49991813007/

21 newburghedinfo, "BOE 6-28-11 Attendance Statement," July 1, 2011, Youtube video, 9:07, https://www.youtube.com/watch?v=hx_4eMgg800

22 Ibid

23 newburghedinfo. "BOE 11-29-11 Full meeting." December 1, 2011, Youtube video, 1:58:27. https://www.youtube.com/watch?v=0C-S3KXnPcDg, clip starts around 49:45

24 Ibid

25 Ibid

26 newburghedinfo, "NAACP 11-03-11," clip starts at 22:44

27 Ibid, clip starts at 15:15

28   "Dawn Fucheck," Ballotpedia, https://ballotpedia.org/Dawn_Fucheck

29   "Natan Vesely," Ballotpedia, https://ballotpedia.org/Nathan_Vesely

30   Justin Rodriguez, "NFA hoops star aims for college," *Times Herald-Record,* August 22, 2011, https://www.recordonline.com/article/20110822/news/108220327

4
GUARDED LIVES
FALL 2017 - SUMMER 2018

I n 2017, a special education teacher emailed new attendance record abnormalities to the BOE.[1] Around the time he finalized grades for the 2015-2016 school year, he discovered a student-athlete in his class was ineligible to compete in sporting events because she had too many unexcused absences. He soon emailed the BOE, which I have permission from the teacher to share. "On June 11, 2016, I reported to my school principal that two of our students/athletes were presently competing while they were ineligible as per our attendance policy. Both students were in my English class for the 2015/2016 school year. I noticed the discrepancy as I was preparing to calculate grades for the fourth marking period (fourth quarter). No one responded to me." Although no one answered him, his complaint was heard. "As I was entering final grades that same week, I noticed a discrepancy in the attendance records of the very same student that I reported for participating ineligibly. When I reported the infraction on June 11, she had 31 unexcused cuts. On June 23, she only had 16 unexcused cuts. She had two full days of unexcused absences expunged from her records by an assistant principal [on] May 2 and May 13. This was done through 'Administrator Approved Circumstances.'" When the teacher spoke with the school's attendance office, he concluded, "Kids weren't going to class and it wasn't being monitored by the coaches nor the athletic director. [...] I believe attendance is out of control."

Little did the special education teacher know that his work would have a profound impact on his community. Not getting much of a response back, the special education teacher turned to the local county district attorney (DA) for help in July 2017. Like his prede-cessors, he did this with the best interest of his students in mind because he wanted them to receive an education. His office orig-inally called the NYSED to ask whether they would look into it. The DA doesn't usually investigate education-related matters, but the special education teacher already sent the NYSED evidence ear-lier in May. They did not respond to any of his emails other than to confirm that the department received them. While I could not review the evidence for myself, he apparently attached evidence that frightened the DA. He later responded, "When this case was originally brought to our office, my first response was: 'Where's the State Department of Education? Where are the people who are supposed to monitor this?' And when it was brought to me after a few times, it was brought by an investigator who said, 'Well, I know we don't get involved with education, but there's a problem here.'"[2] Without waiting for state aid, he subpoenaed the district to inves-tigate attendance problems dating back to 2012.[3] All he had to do now was review the evidence that came in over the course of the school year.

As all of this evidence was reviewed behind the scenes, I was still helping the Mock Trial team out. During the winter months, I also joined a school tech team to repair malfunctioning equipment around the high school. Sometimes I had spare USB drives with me to reboot one of the computers, and other times I was in another room assembling laptop carts for the incoming underclassmen. I easily became one of the busiest students out of everyone, if you factor in everything else I was doing after and during school. Believe it or not, I was actively part of five different after school programs. Learning how to handle all of that work allowed me to forge con-nections with people who I still get along with today. One of the teachers who I met during that time was willing to contribute to this book. Without going into too much detail about the NECSD specifically, I wanted to learn about the importance of the DA's investigation by understanding where the struggling students end up after high school. As of today, Newburgh is still consistently labeled one of the most dangerous cities in New York. With the DA's support, we can break the cycle of poverty by looking into the very attendance problem that is holding students back and contributing to these statistics. What happens when the children reach adulthood? How do they barely get through day-to-day life and "survive" as the teacher told me? These questions must be answered. For the record, some of the quotes are different from what was said in our interview because the teacher wanted to clarify what she said as she edited this chapter.

Like the individual in the previous chapter, her views are her own. I also accept the fact that she wants to keep her name anonymous. She made it clear that she is not interested in being a whistleblower in any capacity, which is consistent with everyone else who spoke with me, because she's more focused on helping students. When the teacher accepted a job at NFA, she told me it felt like home. Given that Newburgh is a poor inner-city community, Newburgh's teachers have tough jobs. The needs of students always varied greatly. She said, "A majority of the students who I've come in contact with are the students who I identified more within school. For me, I found myself gravitating toward students who were struggling, kind of quiet, went unnoticed in school, or not showing up [to class]. I try to catch them and help them be better. There were always the obvious students who needed help. Then, there were the obvious students who succeeded and did well, but a majority of the students I connected with struggled academically and spent time in the streets potentially associated with gang-life."

Most of my friends and I are not familiar with the potential gangs that the teacher described. The teacher said she learned the hard way that you don't even need to have direct ties with gangs to be affected by them. "Newburgh students were involved in the shooting at a Halloween party where two young women were killed," she stated. "One was a former Newburgh student and the other a current Newburgh student with no known ties to gangs or street violence. One rumored theory for that shooting was for suspected retaliation against another Newburgh student. [A male] was the target, but the young women were collateral damage."

Having a target on your back should not be the first thing that comes to mind when you are a student or an educator. "I didn't become a teacher to reform gangs," the teacher added. "I want to help the kid in front of me and show them that they matter, they have value, and they have potential. They may or may not believe that they have potential." One possible reason why they don't have any motivation is because they don't trust anyone. "They don't come right out and say things. They can't as a matter of survival. They live a very guarded life. They don't reveal things until I'm a person that they can trust. There may not be trust and stability in the people in their lives." Just the mere act of sitting down and talking with her is a tough decision for them. "Sometimes, they're so far into a life of poverty that they believe there's no hope for them getting out. But if they show me that they want to do better and be better, then I'm all for helping them. But I don't ask for details about their 'street' life if I suspect they have one because that brings me to a completely different level."

Countless students owe a lot to the professor. She said, "I would usually connect with the students that are eighteen or nineteen and still have at least a year of high school to finish, if not more. A lot of the students that I keep in contact with now ended up being twenty or twenty-one when they graduated high school. Some of them are now enrolled in college." Even after living in the City of Newburgh for years, they still have hope. "One of them graduated and is twenty-three now and told me that she wants to go to school and do something. I try to keep in contact with them and see where they are." When she used to be a Newburgh teacher, she understood what many of the kids in her class were going through. "A kid who walks in the door and shows up to my class is a win because I don't know what their night was like. Was there gun violence in their neighborhood? Even if they have a bed to sleep in, are they sleeping with siblings? Do they have stable housing?" Gun violence is an actual concern that students deal with on a daily basis, believe it or not. One time, she had a kid who walked into class and said, "Oh! Hey Mrs! I got shot the other day, but I'm here in class."

Despite being behind many of their peers academically, students are held accountable and compared to the rest of their cohort. Students who struggle must still show academic resilience. "Once you get to high school, that is when you are truly accountable for your education," she started. "Pre K-8th grade, you can be socially promoted or passed along to the next grade, especially middle school. You can't be sixteen and in middle school, so they will push you up to the high school in grade nine. So now, once you're in high school, you have to start earning credits. There's no way to be socially promoted in high school." If they manage to earn all of their credits by age twenty, they can enroll in college.

As a result of these systemic problems which can also be found throughout the country, universities have to offer special programs to teach students the skills that they should have learned in high school. From her experiences with talking to college-level instructors, she claims, "The professors complain that students don't know how to study, their level of writing or math is not college level, [and] they don't know how to participate in class. They're just not ready." Most of the students in question are in their mid-twenties because they've been out of high school for the last five years. "Sometimes, life gets in the way. They ended up having kids. They have addiction issues and are coming out of rehab. They have trauma from their childhood that they haven't dealt with."

The City of Newburgh has various social and emotional programs like the one administered at the colleges to help these students. Even with all of these resources, however, communities like Newburgh still have many problems. One has to ask why that's the case. For years, very few people had a thorough answer to this complex question. That changed as a result of an incident in Newburgh that made regional headlines. One late afternoon, about two hundred people filmed a music video in the City of Newburgh. Before its release, one of the attendees involved in the production recorded a special "Behind the Scenes" clip of what they did to produce that video.[4] The individuals in this fifteen-minute long segment were largely teenagers and young adults in their early twenties. Their cars took up both sides of the road. As soon as they saw the camera-man, they were filled with excitement. They smiled and ecstatically ran to him from the sidewalks lining the eroding brick apartments. Kids flashed dozens of twenty dollar bills, hand signs, and cigarettes which they identified as "dope" (usually marijuana or heroin). Once the music started playing in the background, kids immediately migrated from the sidewalks to the street just to dance in front of the camera. The cameraman's presence was a call to action, as one of the kids climbed onto a nearby garbage bin. They moved quick-ly onto the streets to chase another cameraman and appeared to have the choice of entering and leaving the music video whenever they chose. At one point, the teenagers parked a pick-up-truck in the middle of the road. By locking down one of its wheels and then spinning it, the producers were able to generate smoke as a visual effect for their video.

As soon as they stopped dancing in the thick fog, a vehicle behind the truck honked its horn. Some of the kids were startled and turned around because the honking wasn't supposed to be part of the video. This was where it appeared that the two hundred attendees were filming on a public road and blocking traffic. You could see them screaming and laughing in the direction of the onlookers before they ran to a two-way road called South Street. The kids were coming from one end of the road with two red cars and a white vehicle as an accompaniment, while ongoing traffic was trying to get past them. Soon, other vehicles from all directions couldn't move. It prompted someone to call the police, and somehow the news reached a city official. In text messages that later became public, he wrote, "I got several phone calls that there were fights happening on South Street on a Sunday evening, so I drove to South Street."[5] This appearance is documented in both the special "Behind the Scenes" clip and the actual music video. The city official is a very well-known individual in Newburgh. From the actual music video, you can see that one of the lead singers holding the twenty dollar bills recognized him and directed the entire crowd toward his vehicle.[6] They were so excited that you could hear them shouting his name and his specific job role in the city. In case it wasn't obvious enough, the "Behind The

Scenes" video also let everyone know that he was a city official in bold white text because they may have believed he came to support them.[7] The music video shows him shaking their hands.

Although it is also unclear whether the city official encouraged them to stay on the streets, they stayed until the police broke them up and attempted to make an arrest. By then, the producers had all of the video clips they needed. They assembled a four minute video that went on Youtube.[8] Some of the scenes had pistols and semi-automatic weapons virtually implanted in them. As the song gained popularity, someone from Newburgh eventually recognized the city official and thought he was a part of the video. They reported him to the press in early June, and a story was quickly published. While the video producers made a great video for their genre, the official's appearance was accused of supporting guns, violence, and gangs. A Newburgh police detective dismally told a reporter on a virtual call, "He's seen smiling and shaking hands with everybody and did nothing to remedy the situation. The city will never ever get better unless you have people who truly care about the city and truly wish the best for the students."[9] The city official countered, of course, by telling reporters his story about how he was trying to break up fights. "No, I didn't make a cameo […] [I]nstead of it being fights, these young teens were shooting a video. I knew some of the kids, so they literally had the roadway blocked. I, like other drivers, were stuck on South Street as you see. I'm surrounded by the teens in my vehicle."[10]

When more information about the video's production came to light, it did appear that the city official's appearance was innocent. One of my hometown's city officials fell into a bad situation that was beyond his control, yet by the time the truth made it to the news headlines, much of the county already heard about his appearance in the video. The official said he did not give these kids permission to use his image and planned to speak with an attorney. He apparently came through on his vow. Today, the music video now blurs out his face. This experience is one that the city official may never forget, though there was some good that came out of it. We now have a good idea of what happens to some of the city's youth after they graduate. I talked to the teacher about this event to get her thoughts. Her immediate reaction to the music video was, "I recognized students. That's the first thing. I didn't watch the video in its entirety because it's not a video that intrigues me in any way. I watched part of the behind the scenes of them smoking weed. It was a little slower moving [video], so I recognized more people that way. My initial reaction was that they're honestly all just kids who are trying to survive. Some are more tied up in gang life and, unfortunately, unsavable. Some of them that I recognized from school were savable."

Each of the students she recognized are now either high school seniors, graduates, or high school/college dropouts. Out of those she recognized, a majority of them did not attend school. The teacher went into great detail as she described each of the students, but she asked me to not include information that could identify them. Knowing them well, she revealed that the video was not a random instance of sheer chaos. Their choice to go down this path was years in the making. The teacher said, "They get caught up in a gang life or street life in some way and they can earn more money on the corner. They don't see any value in going to school." As the Behind the Scenes video shows, she is right. One of the kids kept talking about $200k ($200,000), and another repeatedly showed off his $20 bills. They believed that this video would give them fame. When the police cleared the streets, one of them told an officer that their music studio was "going viral." Thanks to the city official's appearance, the actual music video became one of the most popular videos on their YouTube channel by amassing nearly 90,000 views.

The teacher demonstrates that you can have all of these great programs in impoverished communities, as well as plenty of funding. Regardless, my follow-up research shows it all means nothing to the kids if they don't go to school and get the in-school support they need. It is absolutely crucial that they get an education. These individuals are clearly very talented at making music clips, and they should be able to learn how to make better ones at school without creating controversy.

Giving kids what they need to thrive in school is the difference between their success and failure. In order for teachers to help students, the kids need to be physically present in school. When kids know how to use those resources, there would be fewer colleges that invest in extra support programs and fewer kids smoking marijuana, joining gangs, and failing school. That's what makes the DA's investigation so important. He is the one who is going to get kids off the streets and into class before they put themselves on a very violent path that could get them hurt. For students to get this type of help, they must be supported by school building leadership. In fact, the teacher who I spoke with emphasized, "Teachers need to have more connections with their students, and a lot of teachers do have connections with their students. [...] Teachers are asked to do more and more things and are not given the proper time and training to do those things. If a teacher becomes more overworked, they're not going to feel valued for what they're doing. They're going to just barely do their job description."

CHAPTER ENDNOTES

1   See Google Drive.

2   Heather Yakin, "Grand jury: Newburgh school staff tampered with grades, altered athletes' attendance records," *Times Herald-Record*, April 4, 2019, https://www.recordonline.com/story/news/2019/04/04/grand-jury-newburgh-school-staff/5518949007/, clip starts around 2:50

3   Ibid

4   Kira, "Behind the scenes of Problem Khild & Khubbz ~Droppin Video," April 12, 2021, Youtube video, 14:51, https://www.youtube.com/watch?v=XyMym_A4DWY

5   News 12 Staff, "Newburgh's mayor under fire for role in viral rap video," News 12, June 2, 2021, https://hudsonvalley.news12.com/newburghs-mayor-under-fire-for-role-in-viral-rap-video

6   Upstate Groove, "Problem Khild x Khubbz - Droppin | video by @Upstate Groove," April 22, 2021, Youtube video, 3:52, https://www.youtube.com/watch?v=uHwye_IbdlE

7   Kira, "Behind the scenes of Problem Khild & Khubbz ~Droppin Video."

8   Upstate Groove, "Problem Khild x Khubbz - Droppin | video by @ Upstate Groove."

9   News 12 Staff, "Newburgh's mayor under fire for role in viral rap video."

10   Ibid

ARC TWO

ARC TWO

5
A PATH LESS TRAVELLED
AUGUST 2018 - JANUARY 2019

One week before my senior year.

I t was around two in the afternoon when a bus dropped me off at NFA North. My friends, who were waiting outside for their parents to pick them up, had no idea about my meeting with some of the building administrators, but we would have a lot to talk about afterwards. I remember being greeted by the school principal, who invited me into his office. Inside the room was another principal who led what was known as the Newburgh P-TECH program.

Earlier on, I contacted both of them to talk about my plans for senior year. Newburgh P-TECH is a very distinctive tech program within the district. It allowed a cohort of high school students to earn either an Associates Degree in Cyber Security or Networking from a local college at SUNY Orange (OCCC) for free. Every morning starting in my junior year, I would take a shuttle bus from NFA to OCCC and then another shuttle back to NFA in the early afternoon. This shuttle bus was, in fact, the very bus I took to get to North that day. Most people tend to graduate from P-TECH within five or six years, but it is possible to graduate in four. I was on that track.

Still, there were many thoughts on my mind about my future in P-TECH thanks to advice from my guidance counselor. Throughout my junior year, I had gotten to know the counselors very well. I was in the school's Guidance office about once a week for advice because of my extremely crammed schedule. Without my counselor, I wouldn't have accomplished everything that I did. She provided me with good career advice, college admissions tips, and even

information most students don't have access to like how to calculate the GPA on my high school transcript. As we talked more about
P-TECH, she said it was believed for years that P-TECH would make
college admissions easier for its students. However, I remember my
counselor saying she learned that was turning out to not always be
the case. Around the spring of my junior year, the first Newburgh
P-TECH cohort graduated. Most of them allegedly did not get into
their first, second, or third choice schools. I originally found that
hard to believe. The cohort ahead of me counted eels with conser-
vation groups during the week, built houses with nonprofits on the
weekends, and introduced electricity to impoverished nations over
the summer. No one else in the county did any of that.

At the time, I wanted to get as far away from New York as possible and attend college in the Midwest after high school. My parents
didn't know anything that could help me. Therefore, the counselor was my lifeline. Despite the incredible accomplishments of
P-TECH's first cohort, arguments could be made to reject students.
My counselor showed me that universities need to prove an appli-
cant is academically ready for college. You could get As or Bs in all
of the SUNY Orange courses, but performing poorly on the college
entrance exams and other "advanced" high school classes - which
are the primary academic metrics to compare high school students - may convince the admission officers that the college grades
were inflated. So since P-TECH hardly offered any "advanced" high
school classes that juniors and seniors across the country usually
take, I tried finding ways throughout the spring to allow P-TECH
students to take them. Those efforts failed, which is one reason why
I wanted to meet with the administrators. Yet during the meeting,
I learned I would not be able to get what I wanted at North. Reality
sank in. I had no other choice but to ask to transfer to Main.

Saying those words in front of both principals was already bold
enough. No P-TECH student had ever transferred to another NFA
campus while staying enrolled at SUNY Orange due to supposed
scheduling limitations. On the contrary, I learned that all I had to do

was to take my high school classes at another campus and have the shuttle bus pick me up before driving to OCCC.

Although transferring may seem common anywhere outside Newburgh, it is done very rarely in my hometown. Usually when someone leaves, it's for the most serious reasons. With my senior year starting in just under a week, it was a bit more dramatic for me on a personal level. Things happened so soon that I had to leave without saying goodbye to most of my friends. As far as I am concerned, several people at the school expressed uncertainty of my whereabouts after my disappearance. While most students used social media to check on each other, I was only starting to use it back then. Social media is one of those things that people only get if their closest friends have it, and none of mine used it. On the rare occasions when I did visit North during the school day, my friends all thought I was taking classes in the same building as them and just never bumped into me. Others assumed I graduated early. I wanted to tell them where I actually was, yet I always felt very nervous and was reluctant to tell anyone about what my school day was like. The last thing I wanted was eyeballs staring down at me, which was exactly what happened when the rest of my P-TECH cohort found out about the surprise transfer. On the first day, anyone who had a window seat to the right of the P-TECH shuttle bus noticed me coming out of Main's lower lobby. I opened the door exit as the bus came to a halt, and I entered it. "Is Matt a student here now?" they whispered among many other things. Their shock was apparent because it seemed as if I made a radical decision. After all, I was the first person in the program to make such a decision. It was understandably difficult to remove this tension during my first week.

Even though I was a senior, it felt like I was starting high school all over again at the new building. The smallest details stood out to me, such as the sound of the school bell. I had friends here who I already knew going in. They were the first people to ask me what I was doing here. At times when I would rather not walk in a hallway, I met up with them in one of the cafeterias. No one was shy; they were actually surprised. I remember at the end of my first day, two people I knew from middle school tapped my shoulder as well. That started one of many conversations with people I never thought I would have talked to. Half of the people in my classes were people who knew me from middle school. Back then, I wasn't a talker. During the first week, I got a lot of, "Matt! What are you doing here?!" There was so much catching up going on before class, after class, and even in class when there was a substitute teacher.

By the end of September, I was doing great and adjusting well. It was like I was getting the best of three different worlds: (OCCC, North, and Main) because I had to be at each of these campuses at some point in the day. It's not typical for high school students to have such freedom, even in cities, because administrators usually expect students to stay in one building throughout the day. With this newfound sense of independence, however, I was all over the place and could just pop up unannounced at either North or Main since people thought I had classes at times when I really didn't. In the mornings when P-TECH needed me at North, people could actually find me in the cafeteria snacking on breakfast again and hanging out in the school's library like old times. I would talk with my friends, see how they were doing, and enjoy the good moments while they lasted. I was also not required to attend Friday classes at the college. My professor said I didn't have to come since I completed all of his assignments before his deadlines. Those days, for me, created three day weekends. My Friday classes began at seven in the morning and ended two hours later. A good portion of my leisure time involved catching up on homework in a library or dining at local food shops. At the local food shops, I would typically order pizza, bagels with butter, or deli sandwiches. My dessert would always come from either a local donut shop or a vintage antique store that sold really good rock candy. Sometimes during the afternoon, however, I did not order sweets. I would leave school for trips with the school's Cross Country team for races in other parts of the state. We went places as south as New Jersey and places as north as Saratoga, a city located an hour from Albany (New York's capital). My time on the school's Cross Country team gave me the ability to successfully work through the stress for the first time. I never used to believe the studies that claimed how joining a sports team would help someone mentally and socially because I thought it would take too much time out of my day. On the contrary, running since the start of my junior year helped my grades, kept me awake, and more focused. So once I started running, I never really stopped.

Yet October came too soon. Despite how studious I was, my school-work eventually became a burden. I only got five hours of sleep every night throughout the month of September. Compared to me, the other P-TECH kids had it easy. While they only had to fill out worksheets in their P-TECH classes, I had to take notes on an entire book, prepare presentations, and write a research paper. The additional assignments made me feel like a college student because they kept me working near midnight for the first time. As happy as I was spending time with new friends, this consistent stress was perhaps the only downside to attending three different schools at once.

One day, someone from P-TECH reached out to me about whether I was interested in attending an upstate college. She knew someone there who could help me get in, but they needed some information about me (such as GPA). I needed my counselor's help on this one. She wanted to meet her on a Friday, which was still one of my free days. Her response surprised me when she wrote, "I learned so much today that I want to share!"

The following afternoon, school security let me in without a problem. My counselor was working at her desktop. I had never seen her so serious. She wanted me to close the door.

"Class rank came back. You kept your place. You're the valedictorian."

"That's great!"

She continued to scroll through what appeared to be my grades and someone else's grades. I wanted to ask what she was looking at, but I let her continue.

"It'd be one thing if you guys were in the same classes, but you aren't."

I thought she was talking about the salutatorian. I had a good hunch of who it was. We took many of our classes together throughout high school because we were both in P-TECH, yet that obviously changed at the last minute in my senior year. I figured that the counselor's last comment was referring to my transfer.

"Are you saying we were supposed to take the same classes?"

I was right! She turned around and shouted the name of my opponent, who was also from Newburgh P-TECH. "You're beating him by *one-one-thousandth* of a point!"

"What?!" One-one-thousandth? An assistant principal just told my father I was winning by one-tenth of a point in the previous month!

Usually the top of the class is more well-known. However, I kept my grades to myself up until the end of my junior year. One Friday afternoon, a friend of mine said he needed to talk with me. He later revealed that North Campus was unveiling a new honor roll which was going to come out for the first time. An honor roll is a public list of students and their respective quarterly GPAs. He saw our rankings well before anyone else saw it and was completely in shock. When it came out the following week, everyone else was in amazement too. I was the top of the class. One of my teachers told her class in front of me, "Did you guys see the honor roll? He's going to be the valedictorian!"

Back then, I wasn't doing any of the big things that local valedictorians normally do. They always lead community service projects. They host assemblies within the schools. They're Class Presidents, Vice Presidents, Treasurers, or Secretaries of many after school clubs who usually make the news. Due to the BOE's politics, I was more focused on my family and did smaller things around the high school instead. I was a huge fan of the school's math team and competed in math competitions during all four years of my time at NFA. A close friend of mine also wanted me to join the school's astronomy club, so I did that in my sophomore year. We learned a lot about space and even visited a college campus with a working planetarium.

Some high schools name ten valedictorians. The NECSD only names one. Earning this title is a very competitive honor. The fact that we were separated by only one-tenth or one-one-thousandth of a point also made it as nail-bitingly close as it could get. However, the math for determining valedictorian has never been so straightforward. My counselor explained everything.

By transferring, I had an advantage that the salutatorian lacked. Both of our GPAs were around a 101. His GPA was going to drop no matter what because the courses he took which counted toward class rank lacked a five percent curve (in a 5% curve, the grade you earn increases by 5%). In contrast, I was taking an "AP" (advanced placement) Government class. It had a five percent curve because of its AP status, meaning my overall GPA could still increase. For example, if I earned a 100, my new grade would be a 105. Had I stayed at North, the race would have stayed nail-bitingly close because we'd take the same classes with the same curve. It turned out that by transferring, I influenced the outcome of who would likely become valedictorian.

"As long as you have a 101 overall average in Government, you win," the counselor grinned.

Once she said that, I knew the next two academic quarters were no longer just part of any ordinary semester.

Back at Main, my Government professor was playing classical music in the background. He listened to Beethoven and Mozart most of the time. Every day, he placed class notes at the front of the room for his students to take. My friends were still coming from their other classes.

"Morning Matt. Think you can fix my smart board?" the teacher would usually ask.

Almost everyone at the school knew me for my interest in computers (which the teacher liked to call "crack screens"), even big ones like the smart boards ("uber crack screens"). I approached the board in front of the class as my friends arrived. There was an image or website he wanted to pull up for his class lecture again that wasn't appearing. Since the district's technology department crew installed them in all of the school buildings in the previous year as part of their technology revamp plan, they were relatively new to me. Like troubleshooting the district's laptops with their tech team, everything with the screens originally involved making guesses and witnessing what happened. I selected a series of icons and eventually made my way to the settings bar. Half of the time, it fixed his issues.

Since it was widely acknowledged that my dad serves on the Board of Education, I had to contribute toward the class discussions centered around politics and Newburgh. There was a great deal of discussion about Edward Snowden and the Trump administration, and with the 2018 midterm season approaching, politics became more important for me than ever before. I paid attention to both national and local affairs very closely. Whenever I came home from school that October, I could see my father consumed by the same strange sense of dread that he experienced before the administrator's contract extension. It was a feeling I'd become too familiar with. His friends would call him up, and he would reply back in astonishment.

One cloudy morning after I boarded the P-TECH shuttle from Main, police vehicles filled with investigators surrounded both NFA high schools. Men dressed in suits with ties came out with search warrants and started seizing information as the school day was in progress. One of my younger brothers was at NFA North while the raids were executed, though news stories of the events did not reach me until an hour past noon. I was actually at SUNY Orange waiting for a class to start, nowhere close to the raid. Once I returned to Main the next morning, the damage was apparent. In my Government class, it was impossible not to bring them up. We talked about them for half of the class period. Since I was absent from them, I kept my mouth shut. Everyone else heard that the warrants were executed over the absence clearing. Newburgh's attendance problems suddenly became the biggest news story in the entire county.

The DA finished reviewing all of the evidence from the summer, and he was not happy. There was apparently more to the story than just attendance records. Those who fail an academic subject are presented with two unappealing options: repeat the course next year or enroll in summer school. Around 2016, the district implemented a new online, after-school credit recovery program called APEX. Students in danger of failing an in-person class could enroll in this computer-based service for credit accrual and improve their GPAs.

If implemented well, APEX can serve as a wonderful companion to struggling students. School district documents indicated that APEX coursework is factored into a student's quarterly GPA by averaging the APEX quarterly recovery grade with the student's original quarterly class grade.[1] For example, a student with a 50 class average and a 100 APEX score would receive a new quarterly average of a 75. You need a 50 class average and an 80 on APEX to reach the 65 threshold needed to pass. For some reason, the DA found reason to believe that those scores may have been artificially boosted. "About mid-May of last year, we learned of information about the APEX program and that there may be certain issues with it," said the DA.[2] "We opened an investigation there. On October 23, 2018, we developed probable cause that potentially crimes have been committed regarding manipulation and the student attendance records, as well as the APEX program. A search warrant was executed at the Newburgh Enlarged City School District after it was signed by a County Court judge looking for original and hard copy records of attendance records and APEX records."

My dad eventually learned that the investigators were there for more than just executing warrants. The DA needed interviewees. As the warrants were executed, NFA Main teachers alerted my father of the raid by texting him. This was invaluable information for him specifically. Not too long after, my dad was contacted by one of the DA's lead people. My dad was removed from board committees because he believed he spoke too much about the attendance problems in public. According to my father, he told me he was directed to the DA's headquarters to explain what he knew. When he walked past the building's metal detectors and up a flight of stairs, the DA's office was packed. Think of a movie scene taking place in a large corporation with gray cubicles all lined up next to one another. My father needed to answer whatever questions they had in one of these cubicles. The questioning lasted for months.

The tension created by the search warrants took months to fade away in the district. Stories about the raids were in morning newspapers, evening news reports, and on the popular K-104.7 local radio show I heard on the bus to school. For the first time in decades, it seemed as though the local community was captivated by the ongoing quest for justice that was being led among forces from both within and outside the district. What was being hidden? Was anyone responsible? These questions were on the minds of almost everyone I knew for months. While the NECSD may have been working to strengthen its attendance system, it may have already been too late.

With school assignments coming back, however, students like me were once again occupied with work. I would usually go to the food machines at the end of the school's third floor before my first class of the day, which was English. I could type in my student ID and pick what I wanted. Everything was in a bag, almost like lunches moms pack for their children. There was milk and juice. There were chocolate and banana bars. Usually, these snacks got me through the morning. On the day after the raids, my English teacher locked her front door as soon as the class bell rang. All late students were required to get a late pass from the school's main office. She talked with a colleague of hers shortly before class began. I heard her talking about the raids and how the issues that the DA was investigating were no different from the ones in 2011. But after the school's morning announcements, she got straight to her lesson plans and told us a story. She told us the story of a kid named Kyle.

No one knows whether he is a real person. He's more of a legend nowadays. In his freshman year, he supposedly walked home from school with several books in his hands. When he least expected it, his school bullies caught up to him after school and knocked him in the dirt. The books flew into the air, and his glasses landed in the grass. Kyle was driven to tears.

Then the narrator of Kyle's story, who remains anonymous, ran to him after witnessing the altercation. He retrieved his books. He befriended Kyle. They played football together all the way until the end of senior year. Graduation was right around the corner, and Kyle became the valedictorian of his class. He had to prepare a commencement address. When the moment came to begin his speech, he cleared his throat and started with, "Graduation is a time to thank those who helped you make it through those tough years. Your parents, your teachers, your siblings, maybe a coach... but mostly your friends. I am here to tell all of you that being a friend to someone is the best gift you can give them. I am going to tell you a story." He talked about the day that he was knocked down and helped by the narrator. He planned to commit suicide over the weekend, which is why he had all those books. Kyle didn't want his mother to clean out his locker and carry his stuff home. "Thankfully, I was saved. My friend (the narrator) saved me from doing the unspeakable." Gasps echoed through the crowd, with no one expecting him to tell such a story at the graduation. Some of the same bullies might have been sitting in the crowd as they came to understand how devastating their actions were on his life. What happened to Kyle? We don't know. All we were told is that he went to a city called Georgetown for college, though rumors floated around that he became a doctor to save more lives. These were the types of discussions that took place in my English class. My teacher had been working in Newburgh for some time and was planning to retire in the following year. She was familiar with all the problems that ruin kids. Suspensions for vaping. Arrests for fighting. Yet, she told us this story of a successful individual to show us that everyone has their struggles. I don't think she knew I was the valedictorian. Regardless, my English teacher served as a great advisor for me that semester. While she admitted it had been several years since she taught high school seniors, my teacher spent two months helping her class write their essays for college.

Without my English teacher's help, I'd be lost. Transitioning into writing after school was difficult. Most days after coming home from Cross Country practice, I only had six hours to complete homework, eat dinner, do chores, and then draft two or three 250-word "essays" every night. There were many days when I woke up at five in the morning and went to bed at midnight. Despite the time crunch, my teachers and friends were there to support me. By November, I could think more clearly and just write every weekend from seven in the morning to midnight. My family would visit me downstairs with food and cold drinks, only for them to see my focus on the desktop's six different tabs completing work. I would literally have cold, blue craters beneath my eyes. Even after sleeping, I still had them the next morning. By the end of the application season, though, I submitted everything. This would not have been possible without the support I received.

It would take some time to hear back from everyone. In the meantime, I was scheduled to take a final exam in Government at the end of January. Because this test determined who would be the valedictorian, I could tell many eyes were on me. At the same time, I had to look toward the future. I wasn't sure if I would stay at Main Campus for the second semester. I made many friends here who I didn't want to leave, yet most of North still had no idea where I was. I was getting a lot of "Matt, you staying with us?" questions from my friends and teachers at Main. "I'll have to see," I responded. With my Government course ending, it would be replaced by an economics class. It was another course I needed to graduate. I emailed my guidance counselor to see if I could take economics and English at North, regardless of whether they were AP-level. I wanted to be with the friends who I left.

> "The second quarter (second half of the first semester) will be over by the end of the month. The Government Course I went down to Main for will be completed, so if there's any possibility, I might be interested in finishing out my senior year taking economics back at the North campus. Just something to consider since North has been where I've gone to school for the past three years."

"But how?" she questioned. "How would you go between campuses? Do you want to come back here for English too?"

"That would be the only solution. If there's that option, I will consider it."

There were similar English classes to what I was taking at Main back at North. I would just have a different instructor. If North offered economics and English anytime before I had to ride the shuttle to OCCC, then I was set.

"No, there is not. Sorry. There is an economics class 7th period."

"Is there an online economics course I can take?"

"No, sorry. APEX classes are for credit recovery."

I was confused. Surely, there are other online courses available aside from APEX.

"Does it have to be APEX?" I asked.

"Not really. But the class would need to be pre-approved by the district. Online high school is not really real."

"What are some previous courses that were approved of in the past? Who were they made by?"

"Ummmm. None. No classes that I know of. But if you find something real..."

I figured one of the North administrators had a better idea, so I wrote to him. One day later, he replied. *"Matthew, please meet with me to discuss this."*

By now, my final exams were graded. The administrator was fairly surprised to learn of my return when I walked into his office. It was never part of my original plan to suddenly return in the middle of the year, so he could not approve the transfer. While re-enrolling at North wasn't possible, I wasn't upset. I liked it at Main now anyways. I had a good reputation going there.

At the end of our talk, he checked my student records. I remember him saying something along the lines of, "Hmm. A 98 on the final. A 105 average overall. Not really a surprise."

"Is that for Government?" I asked.

"Yes."

"Awesome! I had no idea!"

That pretty much put the nail in the coffin. I was over the 101 average that my guidance counselor said I needed to become the top of my class. According to her math, my opponent had no way of beating me. Now, I needed her to confirm in writing that no other courses in the second semester counted toward class rank. I really wanted a direct answer.[3]

> *"Does third quarter (first half of the second semester) contribute to class rank?"* I emailed the counselor.

> *"Nope. It is calculated only by final course grades."* She confirmed her initial statement.

Final course grades meant all of my classes up to the first semester (first and second quarter). Nothing in the second semester counted toward the class rank because those classes would be considered "in-progress courses," meaning I was still taking them. I was good to go. It was official. Valedictorian was something I put four years of work into, and it had just been confirmed that I won the title. My mother was waiting outside the school to drive me home, and I'm sure you understand how I felt.

There was no celebration when I returned to school because I didn't tell anyone about what I achieved, but I did walk into AP Government with a smile when I noticed something in the right hand side of the classroom. Earlier on, I took wood burning tools and carved an American flag on a piece of log as a thank you gift to my Government professor for answering all my questions. At one point in the semester, I would visit his classroom every morning to get clarification on what he taught in class. While other professors would have likely been annoyed, he was very content. He was also one of the last Vietnam War veterans in the high school, so he put the log on display next to the school's American flag in his class-room. On that same day, he revealed everyone's final exam scores. My friends were all asking me what I earned. When I told them, we all laughed because - at that point - I knew some of the other students were aware of what I accomplished.

At the beginning of the year, I entered a new school with frustra-tion. I transferred there at the last minute with no one from NFA North even knowing about my whereabouts. Technically, I wasn't supposed to be at Main. With all that was happening, I never would have expected to land in the position I was in. Amidst all of the criticism I received, I made the right decisions thanks to the great support I received at the new campus. It is safe to say that I would not have earned everything I did, had I stayed at North. That is something I will never forget, and more importantly, the best had yet to come.

CHAPTER ENDNOTES

1   Ibid

2   Heather, Yakin "Grand jury: Newburgh school staff tampered
    with grades, altered athletes' attendance records," *Times
    Herald-Record*, April 4, 2019, https://www.recordonline.
    com/story/news/2019/04/04/grand-jury-newburgh-school-
    staff/5518949007/

3   See email in Google Drive

6
UNLEASH THE KRAKEN
JANUARY 25, 2019 – MAY 17, 2019

I f you enjoy learning about the history of World War II, then you have probably heard about Liberation Day. It is a national Italian holiday commemorating the end of Hitler's Nazi regime in the country. In Italy, the day is marked on April 25. In Newburgh, one teacher celebrated Newburgh's own "Liberation Day" on January 25. To the instructor, Liberation Day represented the day when his/her supervisors had to end the "badger[ing], harass[ment], and bull[ying] over the last four years about [their] graduation rate." The teacher added, "They've been cooking the books for four years now. We are the ones who called the DA because we are tired of it."[1]

While the two dates are clearly different, the comparison that the teacher made pertains to how he felt like he was being freed. The DA was back with more search warrants and a battalion of police officers who burst into NFA North and the NECSD's administrative offices as the school day was in progress. People were there, watching law enforcement "liberate" their building's central office. News articles confirmed that the police obtained APEX records and data sent to the Board of Education to supplement the athletic records they took in October.[2] Earlier in the day, FBI agents went door-to-door to the homes of Newburgh's teachers before the DA's raid.[3] Although only one or two teachers may end up being held responsible, witness testimony always connects everyone involved.

Because my father was frequently called into the offices of the DA's investigators, it was crucial for him to know what was going on at the high school. According to information my dad received, one of the lead APEX teachers screamed, "I am not going down for him!

I only did what he told me to do!"[4] "He" is likely referring to one of her superiors. The deployment of federal investigators suggests the possibility that the U.S. Department of Justice opened a larger investigation into the use of online credit recovery in New York public schools.[5] Other towns appear to be doing the same thing as the DA by examining their respective school district's use of APEX. In the preceding months leading up to the raid, communication was sent to a division of the U.S. Attorney's Office revealing information coming from the nearby city of New Rochelle.[6] A school principal allegedly directed staff to alter school transcripts using white out and a typewriter, students "passed" an entire semester in a few days, officials with a documented history of fraud were being hired, people received credit accrual without the knowledge of the teacher's union, and no-shows to class were suddenly registered for online credit recovery programs.[7,8] People have been prosecuted as the feds continued to discover new ways that New Rochelle broke the law, a very telling sign of what would soon happen in Newburgh.

The biggest question surrounding the FBI visiting NECSD employees was whether their unexpected arrival pertained to either the DA's raid or a much larger crackdown at ending the APEX/attendance scandals in New York altogether. The second round of search warrants could provide much more information to the investigators than the first round. They were likely going to have the grades that the students earned in the APEX program, as well as the grades that NFA actually gave to the students. If the two data sets did not match up, it supports the idea that someone must have gone into the APEX and altered the grades which APEX automatically assigned to students. A teacher texted my father to sum up how the NFA staff felt about the warrants. *"This is our last best chance to make positive change in this school system and community."*[9]

Believing this investigation would bring positive change to the school system, a county court judge assembled a grand jury to hear all of the evidence against the NECSD regarding the ongoing attendance/APEX investigations under New York State Criminal Procedural Law.[10] My dad was made to testify as a key witness. He was told that he would be granted immunity from prosecution while testifying to prevent him from facing retaliation for speaking out.

Unlike what many believe, my father wouldn't have testified if it weren't for what my family went through. Appearing before the crowd of jurors in the courtroom was the result of a combination of several events: the controversial nature behind an administrator's contract extension, harassment at the board meetings, discussing evidence of fraud at board committees and then interestingly getting kicked off those committees, interacting with the DA, and the FBI visiting homes of teachers. The DA's investigators sat him down at a desk in the front of the courtroom. For hours, he stayed there answering the investigator's questions. He shared many personal stories with the jury.

Over the next six weeks at the trial, fourteen other key witnesses provided the grand jury with more than nine-hundred pages of testimony.[11] They also submitted thirty-one exhibits, items that supplemented the tens of thousands of data entries extracted from the raids.[12] The witnesses are referred to as Witness A, B, C, etc. in the grand jury report, so I will do the same. The grand jury agreed with the witnesses that the severity of Newburgh's chronic absenteeism problems is causing hundreds of students to miss school and illegally participate in New York state competitions. From one-hundred athletes randomly sampled by the DA, about 65 of them missed an average of over one-hundred scheduled classes annually.[13] Some of these individuals accumulated 400 absences, while others had over 1,500.[14] According to court testimony and the district's Student Attendance Policy, a student can only miss a class if they submit a written excuse (such as illness) to the school within five days of the absence.[15] As long as the students attend each of their classes ninety-three percent of the time every academic quarter, coaches let them compete.[16] Coaches "shall be responsible for monitoring student attendance of the students participating in the particular activity(ies) and ensure compliance with this policy."[17] It is a decades-long custom, based on one NECSD employee's ("Witness B's") recollection, to find dozens of student-athletes on the morning of a major game looking to modify their unexcused absences at the last minute.[18]

Once a sports season ended, the absence clearing ceased. It is clearly visible from the figures in the DA's report. As Exhibit 1 presents, the basketball team members had documented, unexcused absences after the season ended. Yet, they had zero unexcused absences during the season to qualify for state championships. Erasing the records and permitting certain students to play allowed the district to receive positive press. The Hudson Valley Crime Analysis Center supported this claim by associating individual attendance records of outdoor track, soccer, baseball, football, and wrestling players with the press coverage they received between 2014 and 2017.[19] Despite how many of them were ineligible to compete based on the school's attendance policy, NFA had been hailed by the media for its athletes that scored an incredible number of touchdowns, home runs, etc. No one in the investigation had anything against the kids. Rather, one of the later witnesses said, "We should all be ashamed of ourselves, and... we are sitting here again six years later after that basketball investigation and we are looking at the same thing."[20]

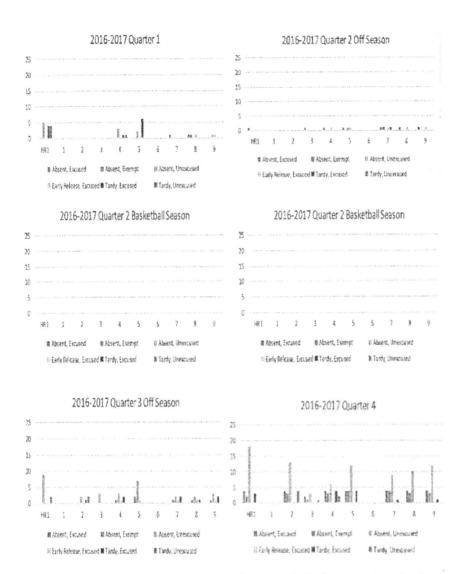

Exhibit 1 -- Figures depicting absences of a basketball player in the school year 2016-2017 divided by quarters and the basketball season. See the full DA's report for more examples. https://talkofthesound.com/wp-content/uploads/2019/04/investigation-of-the-newburgh-enlarged-city-school-district-grand-jury-report-march-29-2019.pdf

While the BOE announced there were no attendance issues in 2017, the report said otherwise.[21] Witness B said the problem always "falls on deaf ears" whether you work at either the administrative-level or the teacher-level.[22] This problem, from the witnesses' perspective, appeared to be systematic. When the DA hosted his first press conference about the malpractices, he summarized the investigation's outcome with the following: "In this report, there will be no criminal charges stemming from this as I said earlier. No one individual or one group of individuals could be identified as being solely responsible for this. This was systematic top-to-bottom."[23]

A grand jury can issue three types of reports. Given the circumstances, they chose to provide professional recommendations from a fact-based, neutral perspective on how to govern the schools better.[24] It was the least punitive of their three choices. Their report is a ninety-page summary of what the twenty-three grand jury witnesses all agreed upon after reviewing tens of thousands of academic records, making it (back then) the most in-depth, eye-witness report ever published about NFA. The grand jury wrote that the NECSD possessed "virtually limitless manipulation of student-athlete attendance records in order to conceal violations of Newburgh Enlarged City School District attendance policies" and "obfuscation of the chronic absenteeism among the Newburgh Free Academy student body that went unremedied for years."[25] On the same day this report was published, the school's athletic director demanded to know the names of students who were ineligible to compete.[26] His tone came off rather harsh to one of the coaches. "For some reason, you seem to be attacking me, and this is not the first time," the coach defended himself.[27] "I'm not sure what I have done to be treated this way. In all my years of coaching, I have never been treated by an athletic director in the way that you have treated me."

The fact that the attendance problems were obvious caused a New York Senator to comment, "On a scale of one to ten, ten being the most troubling, this is a ten as far as school district operations go."[28] Much of the other public feedback on this report is similar to the feedback from the 2011 basketball investigation. Yet as important as attendance records are, APEX provided more insight into the district's educational process because it was also susceptible to misuse. By design, APEX is a good program with features that safeguard against academic dishonesty. According to Witness I, an APEX

Online Learning senior employee, the software company offers training and free resource guides to school districts on how to properly use their service. Areas of suspected academic dishonesty on APEX include "unusually short assessment durations," "large numbers of teacher-entered scores for computer-scored assessments," "low scores on first and second attempts combined with high scores on a subsequent attempt," and "sudden increase in scores."[29] To limit fraud, APEX Best Practices can be modified in the software's settings tab to ensure that questions for computer-scored assessments are randomly selected, quizzes should be retaken up to three times, and the correct answer should be hidden when a student views their score.[30] These settings can also be disabled. Sometimes teachers want to use APEX to help their students prepare for exams, not for credit recovery, so it doesn't make sense to keep the security features on. However, it seems the Board of Education never created policies that outline how to regulate its usage. When students took pictures of their assessments and shared them on the Internet, Witness K (an NECSD teacher) - for example - proposed that building administrators should institute a "no phone" policy.[31] It never happened. The report revealed that the proctors were left to govern the program with unofficial rules.

Because school administrators did not establish enough policies on how to use APEX, lower level employees were empowered to run the program as they saw fit. While many would expect the student's final APEX grade to be the score that APEX reports, the report reveals that the final APEX grade entered into the software is user-inputted by one of several teachers who oversee the APEX program at the high school.[32] An instructor can raise an exam score for any reason, even if the student never took the test. Between 2016 and 2018, hundreds of APEX records were overridden to boost student GPAs months after they took the class.[33] One instructor manipulated 99 records, another altered 275, and a third falsified 325.[34]

Based on these conclusions, Exhibit 2 below demonstrates how easy it became to pass.[35] Regardless of whether they attended an in-person course, a small excerpt of the data collected shows over one-hundred students completed APEX's curriculum in less than two hours with a passing grade of 65 or above. Some people scored a high-90 on APEX within 18 minutes. Many of the grades came from the program's quizzes. According to Witness I, "a student generally has the ability to reset a quiz several times on their own."[36] This means that a student could retake a quiz repeatedly until they scored a 100. "There is always pressure to graduate," one employee testified.[37] "[B]ut, yes, fourth quarter, when everyone is emailing you, guidance counselors are showing up, 'where are they, how far are they in the [APEX] program, are they going to graduate? We have numbers. We need to know' Yes, there was lots of pressure." APEX, despite the creator's best intentions, was manipulated as "something to raise that grade, to get them to that [graduation] field, but the education isn't supposed to come from this program per se."[38]

School Year	Classroom Name	Student First Name	Student Last Name	Time Spent	Final Grade
SY 16-17	QR3 Field Biology			0:16	90
SY 16-17	QR3 Field Biology			0:17	87
SY 17-18	QR3 Pre-College Algebra			0:17	90
SY 16-17	QR3 Field Biology			0:18	77
SY 17-18	QR3 Pre-College Algebra			0:18	98
SY 17-18	QR3 Pre-College Algebra			0:20	81
SY 16-17	QR2 English 12A			0:25	96
SY 17-18	2018 SS English 11 231 Brescia			0:27	70
SY 17-18	17-18 Field Biology Q1			0:29	87
SY 16-17	QR4 English 12			0:29	78
SY 16-17	QR4 English 12			0:30	78
SY 17-18	17-18 Field Biology Q4			0:31	96
SY 17-18	17-18 Field Biology Q1			0:33	80
SY 16-17	QR3 Field Biology			0:33	80
SY 16-17	QR3 Field Biology			0:36	83
SY 16-17	QR3 Field Biology			0:37	90
SY 16-17	QR4 English 12			0:39	85
SY 17-18	QR2 English 9			0:40	89
SY 17-18	17-18 Field Biology Q3			0:41	99
SY 16-17	QR3 Field Biology			0:41	70

Exhibit 2 -- Statistics of APEX courses completed by students showing the school year, course name, time needed to complete the course, grades, and the passing status. More data can be found in the grand jury's report.

These revelations explain why much of the city's population remains uneducated. The DA's findings are upsetting, but he spoke on behalf of everyone who accepted that this abuse of online learning is not what education should look like. He said at his press conference,

"I would note that in the course of the investigation, we did find numerous instances of teachers and other[s] who made personal sacrifices and went well out of their way to see certain individual students had unique opportunities, whether it was to participate in sports or to participate in the classroom, and did everything they could to possibly allow these students to graduate. Some of the facts that you will see in the report are extremely disturbing, and they cry out for something to be done."[39]

Hearing the cries, politicians began pressuring the NYSED to implement the grand jury's recommendations. A local State Assemblyman told the media, "It's very troubling because, if this was happening, it's a great disservice to the students involved because they're really being undercut in having a proper education."[40] Since 2017, the DA's office requested to develop its investigation alongside the NYSED after receiving the initial complaint from the NFA teacher.[41] His office scheduled meetings, left voicemails, provided briefings, and invited them to testify as to whether they looked into his concerns. "I think something has to be said about the fact that no state agency took action in this," the DA continued. "It had to be us. This information would not be public if it weren't for the district attorney's office. While I am not pointing the finger on anyone about that, this isn't anything new that we didn't know about Newburgh based on previous [newspaper] reports of almost half-a-decade ago. I think that this report sheds a lot of light on what has happened in the district during those years."[42] Thankfully, one of the local state senators was able to contact the Commissioner of Education to get her response. During their conversation, he got the Commissioner to admit for the first time that her office mishandled concerns of taxpayers and teachers.[43] The NYSED planned to conduct an audit into the NECSD's attendance policies from 2017 to 2019. In a letter sent to the superintendent that was later publicly released, its objectives were to evaluate whether Newburgh's policies follow New York State Regulations.[44] The NFA special education teacher who contacted the DA and went public with his identity cheered, "I am happy that it seems that everybody is invested in this and invested in our kids to make sure that they are getting the best possible education they can get. That was always my goal."[45]

With the real work just beginning, the NECSD needed help. Just because the state ordered an audit didn't mean the NYSED would reform Newburgh's education right away. My father worked around the clock to implement the grand jury's recommendations. I always saw him late at night reading messages from community members before upcoming board meetings, which became very crowded. Those who spoke before the BOE called the scandal a "travesty" and highlighted how the years of denying a problem existed blocked attempts at creating a better education.[46] They wanted policies enforced, APEX defunded, and for local officials to keep the recent promises they made about fixing Newburgh's education system. Around the same time, the NECSD pushed back against allegations of wrongdoing by releasing a powerpoint presentation that highlighted what was not covered in the report. It revealed that several social workers and attendance aides were hired between 2017 and 2018 so the district's attendance system could be better monitored. Quarterly meetings were also held with each school principal and these attendance staff members to discuss class attendance. They vowed as part of their future best practices to keep better logs of student activity on APEX and possibly consider an alternative solution for online credit recovery if problems persisted.[47]

While many people discussed the APEX/attendance revelations among themselves at the high school, I could not talk about my thoughts on what was going on. Participating in the conversations, as a board member's son, was not always considered appropriate. Amidst all of the chaos in Newburgh, I still attended my courses at Main and SUNY Orange before eventually driving home after school. During the last semester of my senior year, I began to do a lot more volunteering work with the college's Board of Activities (BOA). They taught me the importance of community. While the P-TECH shuttle brought all of the other seniors back to NFA North, I stayed on the campus to host and plan out movie nights, raffles, bingos, and other celebrations that brought the college together. On the weekend before my eighteenth birthday in June, we all went out for a three-day camping trip in a cabin and told stories alongside a campfire with hotdogs, fried oreos, and marshmallows underneath the stars. The timing just happened to work out, and we were a somewhat close group. To this day, my experiences with BOA are what I think about the most when I reflect on my time at SUNY Orange.

When my final exams came to a conclusion at SUNY Orange, there was nothing else for me to work on. This marked the beginning of the end of my four-year trek through high school. Late one evening, I was invited by two middle school teachers, both of whom I hadn't seen in a long time, to speak with their classes about my high school experiences. I agreed to meet them. Walking through the front entrance, the building was the same as when I left. It was almost as though nothing changed, which for me is usually a good thing. I knew exactly where to find the classrooms I was supposed to speak in. I revealed that I chose to take classes at Main days before the NECSD reopened, despite being a P-TECH student. Many people thought that what I did was impossible. Making this call was the toughest choice I ever made up to that point in my life. Looking back at it, it was by far the best decision I ever made.

My family has an annual tradition of stuffing candy and other gifts in baskets for each other on Easter. That Easter, I put a letter in my parents' baskets. Both of them gasped as they read it while I sat on our living room couch. The letter was about a scholarship that I applied for, which was funded by the Bill and Melinda Gates Foundation. Out of the 37,000 U.S. seniors who applied, I was one of its 300 recipients. The essays I submitted for that scholarship would not have been as strong without the help of my senior year English teacher. According to their website, I would receive funding for the full cost of my college attendance. That fall, I planned to attend Columbia University - the Ivy League institution located in New York City - as a computer engineering major. I am the first person in my immediate family to enroll at a four-year college. The college is ranked as one of the best in the world for computer science. When I emailed my guidance counselor, who was actually in New York City at the time, about the news, she told me she drove by the institution, rolled down her window, and shouted, "Look out Columbia! Stridiron is coming!" One of my younger brothers told me that people yelled similar cheers at NFA North down the hallways.

In May, I was invited back to NFA North for a third surprise. The principal wanted to meet with me. I found the salutatorian sitting in a chair outside his office. After waiting for five minutes, NFA North's principal came out of his office, shook our hands, invited us both to come in, and closed the door. The P-TECH principal was inside. My meeting with the two administrators was succinct, lasting fifteen minutes at most. The North principal held two envelopes, one for me and the other for my opponent. We opened them. The first sentence of mine read, *"Dear Mr. and Mrs. Stridiron. It is my pleasure to inform you that your son, Matthew, is the valedictorian of the Newburgh Free Academy Class of 2019."* None of us gave off any surprised looks. We knew the outcome for the past five months, but I was overjoyed to finally read the letter. Aside from the title designations, the messages contained information about celebratory dinners later that month. The North principal spent most of his time addressing those before dismissing us. Although my opponent and his P-TECH peers remained silent, the news got out from my end immediately. Much of NFA knew by Friday, with one teacher even posting the announcement on her social media. On the same Friday, the district sent their Communication and Media Staff to NFA North for official valedictorian photos that would appear on the district's website. The salutatorian and I took many of them by the front steps with the principals of NFA North, Main, and P-TECH. Individual photo-ops continued for another two hours elsewhere in the building, including the library's computer room, which is a place I visited all the time as a junior. Having a picture of me sitting there with my left arm on a desk was, I suppose, fitting for a computer engineer student.

I'll take a quote from one of SUNY Orange's displays to summarize the last four years: "A champion is not defined by their wins but how they can recover when they fall." My family faced overwhelming burdens that would have easily withered away the morale of many other people, but what we experienced is a testament of what a family can do when they just stick together. Every time someone or something drew us into a politically dangerous situation, we showed courage and ingenuity beyond anything that I could have imagined. Politics made us stronger people, and it was believed that the whole community would benefit from the investigation which my father was drawn into. I was ready to move on from P-TECH and NFA while hoping the NECSD would do better for its students in the future. Yet, I also knew it would take time for Newburgh to recover. One person asked a good question on social media. "I don't understand how the District Attorney can do this big investigation - give people immunity and quote them anonymously - and write a scathing report when - in his words - there was no criminality. Is this what the DA does?"[48] The public acknowledged that having these people run the district after they got caught carrying out malpractices is concerning. Once the special education teacher contacted the DA and the NYSED about attendance problems, the district demoted him from teaching at NFA. He now serves as a fourth-grade English teacher. The teacher told the press, "One hundred percent I believe they took action against me because I spoke up. To me, it's not even debatable. I've been in the district for twelve years with a reputation of building the girls basketball program up, and all of a sudden I have all these issues after I reported the attendance. I did things the right way and they went after me when they kept hiring back people that did not do the right thing. I've had to live with that for three years."[49] Despite how he wanted to help future NFA graduates, speaking out did not put him in a better position.

Knowing what could happen to my father, my family monitored social media to make sure no one was plotting anything malicious against him. He is referred to anonymously as a board member and Witness D in the grand jury report, but many of his supporters in Newburgh who watched the BOE meetings knew that he was the only board member who questioned the attendance policies.[50] From what we observed, none of the posts made by the district's supporters that complained about my father were out of the ordinary except for one. This exception mentioned the Board President and Vice President, and it took an unprecedented attack against me (Exhibit 3). The user identified themself as "Realist" and created a fantasy based on very confidential information that I only told a few people about. According to them, my father had supposed knowledge about the "ins and outs of scheduling" and is thus the sole reason for my success. Realist also said I wanted to take APEX in the summer of 2018, "get a full-year course done in half a year," and then transfer for a "shake at being Valedictorian." I think Realist was referring to when I transferred in the fall due to the lack of classes at North, completed AP Government at Main, and asked for a transfer back to North because I wanted to be with my NFA North friends whom I was forced to leave. As a note of precaution, my father only obtained a partial screenshot of the entire post before it got taken down. The phrases I quoted are all in the screenshot. However, I saw the entire social media post. Several people also texted my dad about the claims while it was still up. We were both confused about what this user was saying. My father doesn't know the ins and outs of scheduling. He was thrown off the board committees which would provide him with that information. One news reporter texted my father in shock.[51]

"So what's their story? They're all over the place. Are they now admitting [APEX] is a corrupt program or does it help students? What an angry, ugly, bitter person. Hiding behind a computer screen spewing on a blog that only people in the school district bubble look at. I'd like to see that person trying to say those things in public, in front of you. What a miserable person to go after an innocent child."

My dad agreed. He suddenly saw another post written by Realist. "Now they are calling me a Klan member and that I have a token Latina wife and token African-American granddaughter."

"Ok, that's just getting insane. Wtf. As hard as it might be, I would encourage you to stay away from that forum."

He ended up taking the advice. "I will be hiring a lawyer because the ONLY person that Matthew talked to about APEX was an inquiry in July 2018 with [an NFA principal]."

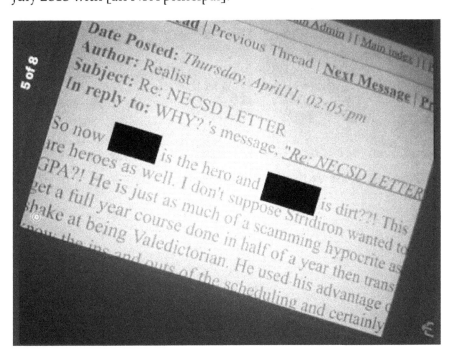

Exhibit 3 -- Part of Realist's social media post in question that prompted attorneys to get involved. The names of the BOE President and BOE Vice President were omitted. While APEX is not specifically mentioned in this image, you can review the entire text exchange where APEX is mentioned on our Google Drive. Because this post has since been deleted, this is the only image my family has.

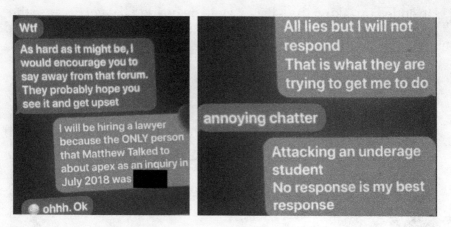

Exhibit 4 -- Responses to Realist's controversial post.

CHAPTER ENDNOTES

1   Robert Cox, "Feds Investigating Apex Credit Recovery in New-burgh Schools, Sources," *Talk of the Sound*, March 22, 2019, https://talkofthesound.com/2019/03/22/feds-investigat-ing-apex-credit-recovery-in-newburgh-schools-sources/

2   Ibid

3   Ibid

4   All text messages can be viewed in the Google Drive.

5   Cox, "Feds Investigating Apex Credit Recovery in Newburgh Schools, Sources."

6   Ibid

7   Ibid

8   Robert Cox, "Abuse of Credit Recovery Programs at New Ro-chelle High School," *Talk of the Sound*, December 10, 2018, https://4a0izvbtoyv1k7lcd14x3s61-wpengine.netdna-ssl.com/wp-content/uploads/2018/12/US-SDNY-AbuseofCreditRecov-eryPrograms-NewRochelleHighSchool.pdf

9   Text messages can be found in Google Drive.

10   Orange County Court Grand Jury Special Term 1, Orange County: Orange County District Attorney, 2019, https://talkofthesound.com/wp-content/uploads/2019/04/investigation-of-the-newburgh-enlarged-city-school-district-grand-jury-report-march-29-2019.pdf

11   "District Attorney Hoovler Announces Release of Grand Jury Report Regarding Newburgh Schools," *Orange County News*, April 4, 2019, https://www.orangecountygov.com/CivicAlerts.aspx?AID=612&ARC=863

12   Ibid

13   Orange County Court Grand Jury Special Term 1, page 51

14 Ibid

15 Ibid, pages 8, 44

16 Ibid, page 12

17 Ibid, page 12

18 Ibid, page 49

19 Ibid, pages 13-14

20 Ibid, page 1

21 Ibid, page 43

22 Ibid, page 45

23 Heather Yakin, "Grand jury: Newburgh school staff tampered with grades, altered athletes' attendance records," *Times Herald-Record*, April 4, 2019, https://www.recordonline.com/story/news/2019/04/04/grand-jury-newburgh-school-staff/5518949007/, clip starts around 28:40

24 Ibid

25 Orange County Court Grand Jury Special Term 1, page 2

26 Justin Fedich, "Ineligibility report has Newburgh athletic officials playing dodgeball," *Times Herald-Record*, April 12, 2019, https://www.recordonline.com/story/sports/high-school/2019/04/12/newburgh-playing-dodgeball-about-report/5444699007/

27 Ibid

28 Lana Bellamy, "Who's accountable for Newburgh schools scandal?" *Times Herald-Record*, April 5, 2019, https://www.recordonline.com/story/news/2019/04/06/who-s-accountable-for-newburgh/5518487007/

29 Orange County Court Grand Jury Special Term 1, page 64

30 Ibid, pages 61, 64, 68

31 Ibid, page 79

32 Ibid, pages 67-68

33   Ibid

34   Ibid

35   Ibid, page 74

36   Ibid, page 60

37   Ibid, page 59

38   Ibid, page 80

39   Yakin, "Grand jury: Newburgh school staff tampered with grades, altered athletes' attendance records," clip starts around 20:00

40   Bellamy, "Who's accountable for Newburgh schools scandal?"

41   Ibid

42   Ibid, clip starts around 24:30

43   Lana Bellamy, "Skoufis: State Education Dept. admits bungling Newburgh probe," *Times-Herald Record*, April 17, 2019, Contact Times Herald Record

44   "Student Attendance Policy to be Audited by State," *Hudson Valley Press*, May 15, 2019, https://hudsonvalleypress.com/2019/05/15/student-attendance-policy-to-be-audited-by-state/

45   Ibid

46   Lana Bellamy, "Public to Newburgh school board: Solve chronic problems related to scandal," *Times Herald Record*, April 9, 2019, link malfunctioned. contact Times Herald Record for link

47   "Response to Grand Jury Report." BoardDocs. Newburgh Enlarged City School District, April 8, 2019. https://go.boarddocs.com/ny/necsd/Board.nsf/files/BB32YT7636EE/$file/Grand%20Jury%20Response.pdf.

48   See google drive

49   Katelyn Cordero, "Who is accountable?" *Times Hudson Valley*, April 10, 2019, https://www.timeshudsonvalley.com/stories/who-is-accountable,5250

50   Orange County Court Grand Jury Special Term 1, page 11

51   See Google Drive

7
SHATTERED
MAY 20, 2019 – MAY 23, 2019

I waited nervously all morning for my father to send me an email that he drafted to an attorney we found, yet I hadn't heard back from him. I quickly texted him after my classes at NFA Main were over.[1]

"Hey. Did you write the email yet?"

"Sent you an email."

I opened my inbox to review the message. Its contents were very specific.[2]

"The attorney is writing to [the superintendent]?"

"Yes. Do you think it should go to anyone else?"

"Downtown. Considering they're updating the stuff."

"Not sure who the contact person is. Maybe [the assistant superintendent], but I think it goes to [the superintendent]. Then it gets noticed."

"Send it to both. How about the head of Central Office (NECSD's main administrative building)?"

"[The superintendent] is the head of Central Office."

"Ok, then it's all good."

This text exchange took place the day before I received the official letter which named me the valedictorian. The "stuff" refers to my class rank. When we found Realist's social media post back in April, my family immediately started looking for an attorney. Every school district in the county had already announced their valedictorian and salutatorian by then. Newburgh was the only district that had yet to publicize theirs. Once we found one, my family wanted to know whether my class rank or the formula used to calculate class rank was being disputed. We never received an answer, likely because I was named the valedictorian the next morning.

Upon seeing the letter, I knew my honor indicated that some people (like "Realist") would be upset about what I accomplished. It is hard for someone to actually link my father, the valedictorian title, the BOE President, the BOE Vice President, and I all together in a social media post about the grand jury's investigation unless they are closely connected to the administration. I emailed and met with an NFA principal in the summer of 2018 about using APEX as a way to improve my grades in a couple of courses, but not unethically. I did not understand everything about how APEX was being used back then. I also met with the administrator to discuss transferring to Main and back to North. From my recollection, that individual was the only person who attended all three meetings. While this would normally imply the information Realist received would have had to come from a source connected to him, my records indicate that two other officials also knew about some of these topics. The information fed to Realist had to have originally come from a source connected to at least one or more of these three administrators because neither my father nor I told anyone else about APEX.

Regardless of who told Realist about my actions, the post made my father fear that the administration would take my title because of his role in the investigation. Given that my father had legal immunity and wasn't paid by the district for serving on the BOE, he couldn't face employment-related retribution. He instead believed something would happen through his children. The immunity he received would be useless if someone came after me, for example. Yet after reviewing the letter, I told my father that he didn't need to worry anymore. Both of my parents disagreed. My mother said she would not rest until she watched me give a graduation speech in front of my cohort at the June graduation as the valedictorian, which is a custom in Newburgh. They believed that the grand jury's investigation offered the perfect reason to come against my family, which is similar to the fates of other district employees.

For the first time that year, my parents learned one potential reason why the attendance problems are so pervasive within the city. As soon as people start speaking out and an investigation concludes, people face retaliation. Just one day after the grand jury released its findings, for example, an article claimed that a principal fired a sub-stitute teacher.[3] All she did between the release of the report and the time of her firing was ask her supervisors about whether certain students were eligible to take make-up exams under the school's attendance policy. When the media reached out to the district for comment, they never responded. This teacher wasn't alone in her struggle. Another teacher wrote on social media, *"So many teachers in this district spoke up and out! We were ignored and abused. The only reason this [report] is coming out is because of teachers who wanted to make a change despite intimidation, firings, and misplacements."*[4]

Although my parents were worried about my safety, everyone at NFA Main around me was hyped by the previous week's news. On the following Monday, many students at NFA Main saw me as a different person than the one I was prior to Friday's celebrations. Twenty minutes into my English class, my teacher pulled out bal-loons and started blowing them up.

"Matt, weren't you named the valedictorian?" a girl asked across the room.

"Yeah! I saw something on social media about that," another added. Everyone was looking at me.

I nodded to indicate that I was thankful for their congratulations. "Yeah! I just got the title last Friday at North. That's why I wasn't here." When more people talked to me about it, I pulled out the valedictorian letter from my bag. Some people wanted to read it for themselves.

With the balloons all ready, we started throwing them around the room for the remainder of the class period in honor of how we only had three weeks left of high school. I tried to hit a pink balloon on my left and a white balloon on my right at the same time. Not many of the one or two dozen balloons actually popped. By the end of the class period, they were all lying on the floor like a party just ended.

"Make good choices! Learn more stuff! Be nice! Everyone's fighting their own personal battle out there!" the teacher said on our way out as she did every day.

Earlier in the day, I told my AP Government teacher (who also taught my AP Economics class) about Friday's events and how thankful I was for all of his help. If it weren't for him answering my questions every day before class started, I wouldn't have kept my class rank. When I told him that very sentence, his eyes popped. During the first and second semester, I never told him about my valedictorian title in case I lost it. Now, there was no reason to keep quiet anymore. Since my next class was AP Economics, the students there were cheering just like how they were in English. They saw my social media posts. Had I not been enrolled at Main, the school would lack a valedictorian and salutatorian to represent them at the graduation for the first time ever since both honorees would be from NFA North. The class wanted me to stand up on my desk with my arms in the air because they were very enthusiastic, but I just stood up on the floor in case the desk couldn't support my weight. When the room was silent, I thanked them and talked about my very busy schedule later that week. Aside from valedictorian dinners, I was to graduate from SUNY Orange with an Associate's Degree in Cybersecurity. This announcement marked the first time many of them were hearing about me studying at the college. It caught some of them off guard.

Word continued to spread after class at both the Main and North Campuses about who the valedictorian and salutatorian were, even before the NECSD had the chance to post the news on their website. When I saw my ride outside the lower level of the high school, I left for the day. My mom let me drive us home. I cranked up the music and changed it to the liking of my little brother, who was sitting in the back seat of our car. Mom was glad to hear that the students at NFA Main were so happy. They really wanted to see me give that graduation speech as the valedictorian.

As NFA students, my classmates and I were always told by the school staff that one of our primary concerns should be to earn high grades. I've followed that advice throughout my entire academic career. However, I hoped I could finally put that behind me now that I was done with high school. On the morning of the previous Friday's celebrations, my ninth grade English teacher at North asked me to promise her that I wouldn't spend too much time on academics at Columbia like I did at NFA. She knew how hard I worked. She wanted me to explore New York City and believed I could get more out of college that way. I told her she didn't have to worry. That was going to be my plan starting from Day 1. In the meantime, I hoped I could just sit back and relax over the summer. Part of me also wanted to work with my father later in the summer at his land surveying company. We were still trying to figure out the specifics of what I'd be doing. At 10:55 a.m., I read a strange text message from my father. *"Call me now. Urgent."*[5]

"Dad, what's up?" I said the moment he picked up his phone.

"Matt! The district just demoted you from valedictorian to salutatorian! Gather all of our belongings! Gather all of your academic records! We're going down to Central Office in three hours to prove you're the valedictorian!"

"Why did they demote me?" I insisted.

"I just talked to the assistant superintendent over the phone. She's with both NFA principals and said that they worked all weekend to make a new policy that would now include third-quarter grades."

"They can't use third quarter grades!" I shouted. "My guidance counselor sent me an email saying otherwise."

"I know... I know... just gather your stuff. It'll be alright." He soon hung up.

I couldn't believe my parents were actually right. Through just a one minute phone call, I learned the district just took my valedictorian title.

Later in the day, my father confirmed that the salutatorian took my place as valedictorian. My GPA was now less than his by a mere 0.04%. Everyone who I talked with during the past two hours called me the valedictorian, not the salutatorian. Because third-quarter grades were now added to my GPA, I learned that the administration apparently included two courses which didn't initially count toward my class rank: English and AP Economics. Including third quarter grades was crucial to the recalculation. Without adding them, my GPA would always be higher than my opponent's. Once they were added, my GPA would always be lower.

Although the administration wanted us to meet them and prove I was the valedictorian, I didn't think they planned on handing back my title. My parents predicted the NECSD was going to take it over a month in advance, and they were right. I had an email that clearly lays out the district's policy. My mom and I convinced my father to not meet with the district, as we had attorneys. Let them take care of it.

Third Quarter
2 messages

This is a staff email account managed by Newburgh City School District. This email and any files transmitted with it are confidential and intended solely for the use of the individual or entity to whom they are addressed. If you have received this email in error please notify the sender.

The email confirming the district doesn't use third-quarter grades to calculate class rank. This is the same email from "A Path Less Traveled."

Dear Mr. and Mrs. Stridiron,

It is my pleasure to inform you that your son, Matthew, is the valedictorian of the Newburgh Free Academy Class of 2019.

The valedictorian and salutatorian for each high school in Orange County will be honored at the Outstanding Student Recognition Dinner to be held at ███████████████████ ████████████████████████████ May 29, 2019 at 5:30 P.M. You and your son are cordially invited to this dinner.

The dinner selections are: Beef (Prime Rib of Beef au jus), Chicken Marsala or Vegetarian (Eggplant Rollatini). Please call ███████████ by Wednesday, May 15, 2019 ████████████ to confirm your attendance at the dinner as well as your menu selections.

We are looking forward to seeing you and Matthew at the dinner.

Very truly yours,

Co Principal   Co Principal

The letter that was received from the district one week before the events of May 20. If you cannot read the text off of these images, please look at the Google Drive.

Understandably, it took a great deal of persuasion to convince some-one that the NECSD would actually take away my title (especially since they already handed it to me). One week prior, my attorney thought my father was crazy after he explained all of our concerns about the district and the outcome of the DA's investigation.

"That is never going to happen!" he exclaimed.

"I hope it never happens, but if it does, I want you ready."

Thankfully, my attorneys were prepared like us when my father con-tacted them in the morning. The fastest I heard of a New York fam-ily-attorney duo sending out subpoenas and court documents to a school district about a valedictorian case was three weeks. We sent the same documents to Central Office in three hours. In an email sent to the superintendent, the assistant superintendent, the NFA principals, and the Board of Education's attorney, my attorney wrote, "Please consider this letter notice that your failure to immediately reinstate Mr. Stridiron as valedictorian will result in an immediate action filed in the United States District Court, Southern District of New York seeking a TRO (temporary restraining order) to redress the situation described herein."[6] We later mandated that they pre-serve all of their electronic communications, video surveillance at Central Office, phone records, and physical paperwork.[7]

By the end of the afternoon when my dad returned home, two fac-tions formed in the Newburgh community. One of them consisted of those who believed my opponent was somehow the valedic-torian. The other rift consisted of those who knew I was still the valedictorian. Amazingly, word got out very quickly about what happened thanks to my father. NFA North's teachers who contacted my dad were furious at Central Office. A teacher confirmed exactly what we were thinking. The teacher texted him saying, "The reason they only go to the second-quarter is because that's what colleges recognize. Your son isn't calling Columbia and telling them his class rank changed after the 3rd quarter."[8] Another pressed for legal action. She texted him, "Fight it. Sue them. Has to be illegal. I organized a prayer team for your family. We will pray daily until I hear that the decision was put back to its original status. Don't give up faith. You do not walk alone."[9]

That night, I was expected to attend NFA North's Seventh Annual Science Research Symposium. My father now advised against it. He texted me, "We can't go to the high school tonight. Too much at stake here."[10] While I was very upset about what happened to me, I was determined to have these administrators know that I would not cower in response to their actions. I needed to make a firm statement by attending this event, which is where my friends would be giving their final presentations. My father came with me as support, so we left the house after eating dinner and walked to our truck. On my way out, something else happened. My mother looked shaken. While starting up the vehicle, my dad sat his phone in between himself and I as he called a friend about what he learned from a news reporter whom he interacted with throughout the day. They were both relaying information to each other through phone conversations about what they heard was going on at Central Office. He asked me to record the conversation on my phone because he believed that his friend would be astonished.[11] If you do choose to listen to the recording in the Google Drive, you may hear my then four-year-old-brother talking in the background.

"Ohhhh. Wait till ya hear this one!" my father started. "Alright so, this is gonna be a huge blockbuster news story. So [my dad's friend/a newspaper reporter] gets a call on her phone from an unlisted number, or at least a number she doesn't recognize, and she picks it up and the guy goes:"

My dad then described the phone call in his words, based on his conversation with the reporter he had in advance, between the journalist and the person who called:

The person started with, "My name is Joey Johns, and I'm from the Concerned Citizens of Newburgh."

The journalist responded, 'Ok... what are you calling about?'

'Uhh I got a real important thing to tell you.'

The journalist was put on hold for two minutes. He returned promptly. 'I just wanted to let you know that I heard there's going to be co-valedictorians at the high school.'

'Do you mean NFA?'

'Yes.'

'Ok. What about it? What's wrong with that?'

'Well. There's a Hispanic kid who's getting robbed because there's a board member who has his son who's not supposed to be the valedictorian, but is now going to be the co-valedictorian because he's using his influence to get him to be in that position.'

'Oh really! How do you know that?'

'I heard third hand!'

'Ok. Do you know which board member it is?'

'Well. It could either be Stridiron or [another board member] because they both have kids in the school.'

'Well how do you know how they calculate the valedictorian?'

'It's by third-quarter grades! You just have to call up downtown (Central Office) to find out.'

'Ok thank you so much.' She hung up.

My dad said the reporter had a bad feeling about this. She covers Newburgh. She covers the school board. To her, the man who described himself as "Joey Johns" actually sounded like one of the board members. Yes, a voice "sounding" like another person's voice isn't enough to prove that the man over the phone is truly a board member who is using a fake name called "Joey Johns." One always needs confirmation, so she texted my father around ten minutes before we left our house (Exhibit 1). She wanted the board member's phone number so she could compare it to the number that "Joey Johns" called from.

The reporter asked my dad, *"Wow. I am getting calls on this. I think someone just gave me a fake name and tried to twist this story all up. [...] [An administrator] may have given [the board member] my cell number. The blocked calls came at the same time he left a message with our secretary at the [newspaper] office, so it was him. [...] Do you have [the board member]'s number somewhere? I just want to quadruple check."*

Dad sent her the number to verify Joey Johns' apparent identity for the fourth time.

"Oh Darren (my dad)... that's it. That's the number. Jesus." A school board member's phone number was used to contact a reporter!

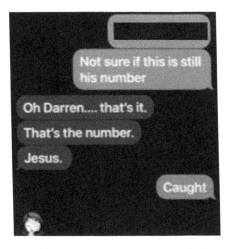

Exhibit 1 -- Screenshot of a conversation where my father identified the phone number that Joey Johns used to contact a reporter. The rest of the conversation is at the end of this chapter.

When dad finished explaining the events, there was silence for a long time as his friend responded. By now, my dad moved the phone to his ear. My phone didn't pick up what his friend was saying. I was in so much shock that I forgot to ask him to put his phone on speaker. All I heard was the noise from the truck's engine as we drove down the road. Eventually, my father shouted back.

"He called from a number she didn't recognize! She looked up the number, and she called him back. He didn't pick up, and she left a message."

The reporter stated, 'Ok. I don't know what game you're playing, but I'm trying to cover Newburgh honestly and you're playing games with me calling yourself Joey Johns coming up with this BS story about valedictorian. How am I going to believe ANYTHING you have to say?'

My dad continued. "She's gonna publish that in the newspaper tomorrow! She's going to do a story on it. She's going to interview my son tomorrow about the story and she's going to put in there exactly what happened with [Joey Johns]."

There was more silence.

"He's first of all saying I'm using my influence to try to change the situation, and a poor Hispanic kid is going to get hurt because of my son and my influence."

"Yeah! He's Italian!" (referring to the salutatorian, though he definitely looks Hispanic too).

There was more silence.

"She got the phone call before they [the district] even gave me the offer!"

"No! They didn't make me the offer yet! That call came in BEFORE they sent me the offer. So, he's down there [Central Office]."

"Yes. Oh yes. Yes, they [the district] wanted a co-valedictorian."

"No. Nonononono definitely not," he laughed nervously. "Everyone's going down!"

"He thought he was blocked! Ahhhhhhh," he groaned, as if he knew that the next few weeks were going to be very rough.

"Well how did he know about the offer before they even made it to me? That means [Joey Johns] is down there PLANNING ALL THIS!!!"

"Yes! She's going to do the story tomorrow and interview my son and put this in part of the story. [...] I mean he's gotta get thrown off the BOE for that. I wonder if I could sue him for that."

My dad talked about potential legal options.

"I already told the attorney we're not going to accept this. [...] No matter what happens, they're gonna pay fees and all kinds of stuff. It's gotta be investigated."

We were nearing North Campus. We would have to sort all of this out later.

"All right man. Bye."

Claiming my dad was abusing his privileges to get me places? Using ethnicity as a means to an end? I sensed a trend connected to Realist's social media post. In seven hours, I went from valedictorian to salutatorian to co-valedictorian. We heard rumors earlier in the day that this change was going to happen, but not like this. Like I said, I didn't have the time to think about Joey Johns. We were almost at the school.

Just two minutes later, I was outside the front entrance of NFA North. The science research program was one of the better programs offered at the high school. It was a three-year experience that connected students to a professional scientific community by allowing them to research a topic of their choice under the guidance of university-level professors. I visited the symposium over the past two years to support my friends. They would be giving their final presentations tonight. When I walked in, the thirteen researchers already had their presentation boards set up on tables throughout the room. Crowds of people were talking to each of them as others waited their turn by eating cookies and cupcakes that sat on a table to the side. I was able to read the titles of some of the boards, and I was so impressed by the presentations that I took pictures on my phone. "Toxicity studies of silica nanoparticles on E. coli." "Veterans and Horses: The Value of Equine Therapy for Returning Veterans with PTSD." Most of the research linked back to biomedical/veterinary sciences. Once the crowd cleared up, I walked to one of my friends.

"Congrats on valedictorian!" he told me.

It's amazing how a seven-minute phone call can completely warp my view of the title.

"Thank you," I replied. I definitely considered myself deserving of the honor after what I just heard. "Actually, I could use a refresher on your research."

He didn't mind. The last time I talked with him was a couple of months ago. We certainly did not mention science! Much of his explanation was technical. He actually went to a university lab to obtain his data, which is apparently a tradition for many of the scholars in this program. Soon, everyone made their way into the school's auditorium. The main event was about to begin. A keynote speaker addressed the crowd.

"Where there's smoke, there's toxicity. Climate change makes it worse," I remember her starting off.

Given that her work resonated with that of the students, she delved deep into her climate change research. Then one by one, the five seniors presented the same topics that they talked about before, only more extensively using their powerpoint presentations. Some of them had to gather bacteria and create an environment where it can grow in petri dishes. At the very end of the program, one final slide was displayed as a gift from the program's sophomores and juniors. I took a picture of it. "Goodbye Seniors!!!!" it read with a sad emoji on the side. "It's amazing how work became fun when you guys were around. You guys were not just classmates, but very good friends too. Thank you for always being willing to extend a helping hand. Your presence will be missed. Good luck in college. We wish you lots of success on your further way. We're going to miss you." The seniors were all at the front of the room having confetti thrown at them by the same juniors and sophomores. This surprise was a good way to end the conference on a positive note - at least before

I noticed an administrator by the stage who I heard was at Central Office earlier in the day.

When I saw him approaching the students, I was filled with rage. Despite the happy face he put on for the crowd, I questioned whether it was genuine. If a board member actually called himself Joey Johns and made up a story about me, co-valedictorian is not something the district intended to offer me. It is something they intended to force onto me, and they thought I wasn't even aware of what they were doing.

While I got the sleep I desperately needed later that night, slowly but surely I woke up to a new realization. That morning began my first full day as a "co-valedictorian." Every Newburgh Free Academy student still thought I was the valedictorian. My parents were already awake in the living room since school was closed. Their friends described Joey Johns and his phone conversation as "complete BS."[12] One of them even said, "'Outspoken BOE Member's child victim of retribution.' [...] Headline writes itself."[13] This particular individual was so outraged that he and his friends called New York senators and reporters who later went to the high school demanding information about my case. The district was already being battered with media requests. The texts say they were "all over this thing."

There's no question that my family was prepared for the moment my title was stripped from me. We just weren't ready enough. None of us expected anything close to the Joey Johns story that we heard. Had the reporter published it without contacting my father, it would have made my entire family look corrupt and destroyed my family's reputation. This dispute was now about much more than just a valedictorian title. The reporter apparently felt so uncomfortable that she was not willing to call Joey Johns back until the following morning when her editor would also be present for the phone call. These text messages clearly show that the reporter understood someone using a board member's cell phone number had contacted her, and the phone call is so outrageous that *Scheming In the Dark* reached out to the NECSD for comment before our official book announcement.[14] While the individual accused of being Joey Johns later had the chance to comment on this story in legal documents, he chose not to. His attorneys instead stated there was insufficient evidence to prove there was any wrongdoing. Furthermore, the reporter's text messages to my father reveal that the person accused of being Joey Johns claimed his nephew made the call. If this is true, how his nephew obtained this information is still uncertain because only district administrators should have been aware of all of the conversations happening at Central Office.

As another layer of precaution, *Scheming In the Dark* reached out to the district's media person because we saw that the district officials wanted their legal defenses to go through the NECSD as opposed to them directly. We also tried learning about the Concerned Citizens of Newburgh, yet it is unclear whether that group actually exists because of their small Internet presence. According to additional text messages between my father and the news reporter that you can read on the Google Drive, Joey Johns received a voicemail from the reporter. We wanted to review the voicemail and all of the evidence from the NECSD's end which could prove or disprove what exactly was said. By law, we are entitled to review that information because the district was sent a litigation hold. We also wanted to know whether the BOE conducted an internal investigation into the phone call. However, the district's media person never responded to our two inquiries.

After looking at the recorded conversation, the text messages, and the district's lack of response to the allegations, here is what Scheming In the Dark currently understands. The texts show that something about my valedictorian title was discussed during the phone call, but we could not verify exactly what was said. Someone apparently called using a board member's cell phone, but we could not verify whether Joey Johns is truly the board member. We don't know whether the BOE investigated the phone call. We don't know whether they preserved the records that they were required to keep in the litigation hold. We don't know who gave Joey Johns the reporter's cell phone number. Despite this lack of information, no one can say Joey Johns didn't do anything wrong because the district wasn't even willing to comment on the story. Had the district's media personnel responded back to *Scheming In the Dark*, we would likely have our answers. It should be noted that the district was eventually given these text messages for reasons you'll learn at the end of the book, allowing them to do an investigation. The district's silence therefore indicates that the phone call's contents stand undisputed as of now.

When school reopened the next day, I wasn't sure what to expect and had to be on my guard. Was I truly a co-valedictorian? I knew that people were still going to be happy about last week's news because they had no idea what happened on Monday. Since all of the graduating P-TECH seniors were supposed to ride the shuttle bus to SUNY Orange's graduation rehearsal that morning, I decided to make the bus driver's schedule easier by starting my morning off at the North Campus. The bus wouldn't need to pick me up at Main. At the high school, the air was filled with excitement. Students were still calling me the valedictorian. "Hey! Congrats on valedictorian, bro. I'll see you at graduation," was one of the first things I heard by the building entrance.

With the school year almost over, the senior cohort had their own reasons to be ecstatic. Senior talks are a rite of passage for students who attend NFA North. Each senior is required to prepare a speech about a topic of their choice after researching it for six months. Although the senior talks are usually held in the school library, they were taking place in the North Campus auditorium that year. It's the same place where the science research symposium talks were given two days earlier. Amidst the noise of the school metal detectors as students still entered the building, lines of students were slowly proceeding into the auditorium with their teachers through the hallway. I didn't have official classes at North, so I had the freedom to sit with my friends. Once I got there, one of them was giving a very personal senior talk about mental health. I looked around to see the clapping in the room. A few seats behind me were two administrators. They gestured for me to come and talk. I didn't want to meet with them, but I promised to do so after the next senior talk.

One of my friends was about to give his presentation about naturopathic medicine, which are cures that combat disease by the use of natural remedies rather than prescribed medication. Watching his speech was more important to me, and I had no regrets staying. I later texted him, "Great job! Your talk was amazing!"

Now it was time to see what the principals wanted. My new legal case was always in the back of my mind. They should have read the legal paperwork by now about the valedictorian dispute. One of the key sentences in the legal paperwork sent to the district was, "Be advised that Mr. Stridiron and his family are represented by counsel. Do not contact them directly."[15] Even if they violated my attorney's wishes by talking about the dispute, I wanted to know the district's side of the story. I walked across the hallway from the auditorium into the building's Main Office to learn whether the first principal returned to his office. He apparently had to get something for me. I started recording everything on my phone in light of Joey Johns' conversation, and since the administrators had the chance to respond to what happened as you will see in the next chapter, I feel comfortable describing that conversation based on the recording. NFA North was bustling with laughter and chatter after the first-period bell rang. Everyone seemed to be having a good time.

When I found the first principal, he was talking with another student in his office. He looked up at me and immediately said he would come with me to the other principal's office within a few minutes. Of course, I asked him why we were meeting. He said he had no clue, though he did congratulate me after he apparently saw me at an awards ceremony for something separate.

Time passed. Eventually, someone walked over and told me that the second principal was ready for us to meet him in his office. I found a teacher sitting by a roundtable as she grabbed her papers and left. Once the two administrators and I all settled down at another table in front of a window where I could see the P-TECH shuttle bus, we closed the door. All of the other P-TECH students were already on the bus waiting for me, but apparently, the driver had special instructions not to leave. It seemed that the administrators wanted to offer their side of the story.

They told me all about what happened on the morning of May 20th when my title was taken away. The principal whose office we were in revealed that he, various principals, and various superintendents all met together about a tabulation (GPA) update at Central Office. After my GPA was recalculated, the administrators concluded that the district had co-valedictorians!

At that point, I studdered. The reporter's call had truth to it! The same principal who told me about how the district created co-valedictorians had to calm me down.

"I'm just... Matthew, let me say," he started.

"Alright, alright. I didn't say anything."

"No no no, let me just tell you everything then you can ask questions."

He proceeded to pull out a letter that was signed by him and another administrator. He said it would give me new information about the tabulation. However, the letter did not mention anything about how my grades were calculated. The letter instead elaborated on valedictorian dinners, the first of which would be held that evening. We talked more about this upcoming event. Not only would the former salutatorian and I be present, but also a third individual who became the new salutatorian. At one point, I asked what the new recalculation was based on. As many people would expect, the administrators claimed their class rank policy was built around third quarter grades. They added my English and AP Economics courses into the recalculation.

"This is unusual," was all I had to say.

Both principals believed that I was talking about how uncommon co-valedictorians are. Yet, I was more surprised about how much of their story corresponded to what I already knew. It's amazing how the administrators may have thought that I was learning some of this information for the first time. We talked a little more before I was ready to leave. As much as I appreciated their time to tell me everything, I felt sick leaving the room for obvious reasons.

May 21, 2019

Mr. and Mrs. Darren Stridiron

Dear Mr. and Mrs. Stridiron,

It is my pleasure to inform you that your son, Matthew, is the co-valedictorian of the Newburgh Free Academy class of 2019. We apologize for any confusion from the letter dated May 13, 2019.

The valedictorians and salutatorians for each high school in Orange County will be honored as follows:

1. The 54th Carroll F. Johnson Scholastic Achievement Dinner will be held on Wednesday, May 22, 2019 @ 5:00pm – ▓▓▓▓▓▓▓▓▓▓▓▓▓▓▓▓▓▓▓▓▓▓▓▓
   Please note that this dinner is for students only. Please see the attached invitation.

2. The Outstanding Student Recognition Dinner to be held on Wednesday, May 29, 2019 @ 5:30pm at ▓▓▓▓▓▓▓▓▓▓▓▓▓▓▓▓▓▓▓ You and your son are cordially invited to this dinner. Your RSVP and dinner selection have been received.

We congratulate Matthew on his outstanding high school career. We are looking forward to celebrating his achievement.

Very truly yours,

Exhibit 2 - The letter that was distributed on May 22, 2019 (the letter is dated May 21, 2019, likely because that was when it was printed). If you cannot read the text off of these images, please look at the Google Drive.

Hours later, the NECSD announced that I was a co-valedictorian on their website.[16] The district's individual schools retweeted the news as if it was some sort of a celebration. They posted the picture of me in North's computer room to make it look like I accepted the title, when in reality, that photo was taken when I was still the sole valedictorian. In previous school years, the district always revealed the students' GPAs on the website. The NECSD removed them this time, thereby preventing my family from seeing my new GPA. Some of my closest friends were probably now thinking that I lied to them. I never said I was sharing my valedictorian title with someone else. The attorney advised my family to stay calm. His legal team immediately filed papers to get a judge assigned to my case and a temporary restraining order on the district immediately.

Over the next two days, many of NFA North's teachers called my father saying I was robbed. They remembered how pizza was delivered to the high school to celebrate my title the week before. Countless individual and group photos were taken by the NECSD's own media staff. We had a party. The faculty really hoped I could enjoy the rest of the week. The last scheduled event of the week was the SUNY Orange college graduation, which took place on a Thursday afternoon. Even in light of my demotion, this was one of the many days I had been looking forward to for the past four years. I would become the first person in my family to graduate from college before high school. One of the P-TECH employees wanted me to arrive an hour before the main event. Several reporters from all over the Hudson Valley wanted to interview me about my high school experiences.

While rain prompted the location of the ceremony to be moved inside the school's gym, most of the heavy clouds were gone by the time we reached the school. My mom left shortly after to pick up my dad. When I walked to the front of the building, most of the interviewers were already talking with the graduating P-TECH seniors at the entrance. The roof of the building extended outside to the front steps, so we were still protected from any potential rain. I just needed to fill out a sign-in sheet inside before I could speak with them. A volunteer at one of the room's front desks handed me a SUNY Orange pin, a name card, and an orange rose - symbolic of the school's colors. I attached the pin to my graduation robe, but I held the rose in my hand. My attire lacked side pockets. Around this time, there were around twelve other soon-to-be P-TECH graduates. We took many group pictures and interviews in the first hour before an NFA principal and two media liaisons, one of whom worked for the NECSD, approached us. The district's media liaison wanted a photo of the co-valedictorians and two other scholars. We didn't refuse, but we'd been in so many that I wondered whether I would be able to keep my smile.

All of the journalists left half an hour before the main commemoration, and the graduates moved into the building. Everyone was divided up into lines based on their major. There were about 500 people in my cohort. As I took pictures of the celebration, I saw some of the students customized their caps and graduation robes beforehand to represent their respective academic departments. One student - who I assumed was an architecture major - built a model house on his mortarboard. Ten minutes later, a woman came out of the gym and into the main hallway. She directed the lined-up students where to proceed, as the celebration would start any minute. When we heard the SUNY Orange band play "Pop and Circumstance," the most famous of all graduation march songs, it was our cue to move. I followed a long line of people down a hallway of classrooms, through another long corridor with empty sporting courts, and a third hallway that leads into the gym. My parents, grandparents, aunts, and uncles were all watching me come into the gym either in-person or through the college's livestream. When I entered the gymnasium, a large group of spectators sat on bleachers located at both sides of the gym. In between the spectators were rows of brown seats laid out for the graduates. Small white fences surrounded them to stop the guests from accidentally sitting in them. I ended up finding myself in one of the last rows with the P-TECH seniors. All of the front row seats were taken.

It took another six minutes for everyone to settle down. The faculty set up a stage in the center of the room earlier in the day for the SUNY Orange President and her staff to give speeches and allow graduates to collect their degrees. My graduation class started throwing around several beach balls that we snuck into the room. At SUNY Orange, it was a tradition. Once the President reached the stage, the music died down. Everyone clapped and instinctively knew to stand for the Pledge of Allegiance and the Star-Spangled Banner. In her speech, the President compared the college's first graduating Class of 1951 to today's Class of 2019. "Nothing now will please us more than to watch you create that beneficial and fulfilling future. For you to discover and apply those constructive solutions that were called for as far back as 1951. To trail the good old days and the ideas that still make sense, and to bring them forward to the environment that we inhabit today, and simultaneously create that bright tomorrow. To witness it, just watch these graduates. I guarantee they will make a difference. Congratulations, graduates. Now let's confer some degrees!"

The President and her spokesperson explained that the students would receive their degrees one row at a time. We needed to come up to the stage, have our name read aloud on a microphone, receive our degree, and return to our seats. It took a while for me to go up. My row was finally called after an hour. I quickly placed the rose underneath my seat and grabbed my name card. People tend to pronounce my last name as "Stride-iron" instead of "Strid-iron." There's no way I wanted the woman near the platform to mispronounce it, so I gave the card to her with my last name spelled as "Str-id-iron."

"Matthew A. Stridiron," she said over the microphone.

She got it right! I collected my degree and shook hands with SUNY Orange's President.

"Congratulations on valedictorian," she whispered.

Twenty minutes later, the room cheered. The last student walked off the stage. A spokesperson reached for the microphone on the stand. "Now is the time I ask you as graduates and as the newest alumni of our institution to please stand. In accordance with academic custom, you may move your tassel from the right to left side of your cap to signify academic accomplishments!" Everyone cheered for a good ten seconds. "Please be seated," she eventually stated.

"Well, congratulations to the Class of 2019," added the President. "I'd imagine you are now also confident that you have graduated from an exceptional college, and you are exceptional graduates."

Three more speakers came up to the podium. It felt as if almost no time passed at all. All of a sudden, the event I'd been anticipating over the past four years came to a close. OCCC's chorus sang one last song as we exited row by row out the front door. We were directed onto a concrete path that led to Alumni Green, the largest grass lawn on the campus. I've walked this path every day since the prior August, yet the length of the pathway felt so long walking through it one final time. Nothing was happening on the lawn by the time I reached it since the grass was still too moist from the rain. Instead, everyone took pictures in the area around the concrete path. After seeing everyone in a good mood, it was hard for me to leave.

My mom and dad bought three pizza pies, this time with garlic knots too, to celebrate back home. One of the first things I did when I got home was fill a glass vase with water for my rose. I placed it next to my mom's plants on top of one of her countertops by the windowsill where it would eventually get sunlight. That night, we planned to celebrate the accomplishments of my second-oldest brother and I. My brother was inducted into the National Science Honors Society while I was at the graduation. We all wanted to hear about our experiences. When it was my turn, I obviously described how I felt when I got my degree. I also told them about one reporter who was very interested in what I had to say. She was very surprised and really wanted to keep in touch with us for reasons pertaining to the valedictorian title and Newburgh P-TECH, which she was interested in covering more of.

In regards to P-TECH, we all understood that the valedictorian title did not just have importance at the local district level. Newburgh P-TECH took it seriously too. Believe it or not, the P-TECH program is a part of a larger global network which was founded in 2011.

President Obama praised the growing success of the P-TECH initiative in a State of the Union address as a model for public education reform. Today, there are over 240 P-TECH schools in America and can also be found worldwide in Colombia, Argentina, Italy, Poland, Mexico, Singapore, the United Kingdom, Hong Kong, and nineteen other countries.[17] From what my family has researched, I am the first P-TECH valedictorian ever to come out of a public high school. After hours of investigating, neither my father nor I could find a news article that verified the existence of a P-TECH student who became the valedictorian of their public high school. The first P-TECH class graduated in 2015. There are only three-years worth of cohorts since then, but we have not found a single person on the Internet who fits the criteria we were looking for. The only ones that we found were those who only competed among their P-TECH peers (basically the smartest P-TECH student) rather than an entire public high school filled with students who are not enrolled in the program. However, we did find a P-TECH salutatorian who graduated from a public high school. Her rival was not affiliated with P-TECH. Taking college coursework puts you at a risk of lowering your GPA, which is likely what happened to the first P-TECH salutatorian. Still, I was one of five people in my OCCC cohort who earned a perfect 4.0 average at SUNY Orange after earning 87 college credits (if you factor in AP courses). It raised my overall high school average significantly because some of the SUNY Orange courses were placed on my high school transcript. Even if my family missed something and I am not the first P-TECH valedictorian, I am likely one of the first. I kept telling my family that if the district had named me using my actual title on their website, my accomplishment wouldn't just be on the newsfeed of my local town. This story could have made the news in many other places. When I was in P-TECH, we had P-TECH representatives from Sweden and Australia visit our classrooms because they looked up to Newburgh specifically. Despite my great accomplishment, we couldn't highlight it because we decided it was more important to check on the people who were most affected by my dispute. My father frequently texted the reporter who heard from Joey Johns to see how she was doing.[18]

"I know for a fact that the rest of the BOE has no idea this is all happening."

"Except Joey..." she replied. *"I mean [the alleged person who came up with the pseudonym]. He called me back today again asking me to let him 'explain' what 'transpired' with the phone call."*

"What transpired? I'm sure your editors will be interested to hear his reason."

"Yeah, [the reporter's editor] thinks it's sad and kind of hilarious how absurd it all is. But mostly just sad."

"Just think, people like [the person who allegedly called the reporter] are making million-dollar decisions for our children."

"Apparently [a local community center representative] called [the reporter's editor] about the phone call thing, which is hilarious. He doesn't want to be involved."

This community center serves young children throughout the week by helping them excel in sports, math, computer science, chess, arts and crafts, and a variety of other activities. *Scheming In the Dark* learned that the individual in question used to regularly visit the center. If what the reporter says is true, the institution would understandably be concerned about Joey Johns' behavior because it serves a large Hispanic and African American population. To be honest, I never learned what was discussed in the conversation. All I know is that after the phone call, the reporter called my dad to say the story about Joey Johns was not going to run anymore. Text messages show that her newspaper was worried about covering the story. At the same time, I was advised not to give an interview by my attorney.

Interestingly, these concerns did not stop her newspaper from publishing an article about the dispute three weeks later.[19] When my second-oldest brother told me the story was on the front page of the newspaper, I was surprised and had just purchased my graduation photos from SUNY Orange's website. We read it together downstairs. While the district's side of the story is present, it omitted almost everything you read in this chapter. It talked about third-quarter grades, but not my guidance counselor's email. It briefly mentioned my father's status as a "whistleblower" (even though that's not how he views himself), but nothing about Joey Johns. It didn't even mention the impact this title had on P-TECH! Instead, this article made my case seem like an ordinary class rank dispute, and almost everyone in Newburgh would later believe that. The Facebook page of this newspaper has nearly 150,000 followers, so my story reached the news feeds of all of these people. There are about 30,000 people in Newburgh. Assuming everyone in Newburgh follows this newspaper (a huge overestimate), the other 120,000 could be from anywhere in the world.

Once other local newspapers wrote a story about my case based on this article, most of them omitted the same information. As a result, we had many people outraged at my family when they shouldn't have been. The Facebook page of Newburgh's lead newspaper was filled with comments and shares. One social media user depicted me as a baby crying and fumbling. Another user took a scene from an Iron Man movie and showed Tony Stark shrugging, as if my honor was no big deal (Exhibit 3). This second individual was emboldened to post this animation upon receiving praise for another post that said, "Really? Come on! Those parents are teaching that poor kid how to be a sore loser." I was humiliated. There were dozens of these types of damaging posts against me that you can see on social media for yourself. What followed was a horrific shaming spree to make me feel guilty over a dispute that I had good reasons to fight.

Really? Come on! Those parents are Teaching that poor kid how to be a sore loser

Like · **Reply** · 2y   23

Exhibit 3 - Public reaction to the article published by Newburgh's lead newspaper. Source: https://www.facebook.com/recordonline/posts/10156597841371298

Remember how the teacher from the chapter "Children Caught In the Middle" said there's no future payoff for living in a cycle of poverty? As this book clearly shows, you really need to use all of your resources if you want to escape this cycle. I grew up around a cycle of poverty, just like my parents did alongside my grandparents. We know that everything adds up. Studies have proven that many people who are named the valedictorian of their class achieve exceptional success in life. The students in Newburgh who genuinely struggled to graduate from high school may scoff at my response to being demoted unless they see firsthand what I went through. Think about the individuals who were also demoted or lost their jobs after the investigation. These people worked hard so that all of the kids in Newburgh could succeed in the first place, and some of them ended that school year feeling like their efforts weren't successful because of this incident and the other negative backlash they received.

I know when to ignore harassment, and I know when it goes too far. May 20, 2019 is the darkest example of when it could not be ignored. No one can change the fact that the district took my valedictorian title, but what I can use it as is a stepping stool for growth. I don't play the victim. I am known for being a very strong person. I've helped many friends overcome depression and guided them when they needed advice the most. Hardly anything can break me, but this situation is different because it hurt my family. My health took a turn for the worse during that week. My relatives reached out to many individuals they knew who claimed to care immensely about mental health, yet most of them didn't help me in the same way that I helped my friends. In contrast to the days when I helped people, this time I was on my own. Although the lead newspaper omitted my perspective, it made it to this book. Today, I am running the story. Regardless of the treatment my family received, I smiled for the photos at the "celebrations," shook the superintendent's hand, and went back to my seat at the events without a protest. My father instructed me, "This is the right thing to do." Looking back at everything, that was the wrong advice. Many people may read this chapter for the first time thinking, "Why didn't Matthew say anything?" To answer their question, my father and I did not know much about legal disputes. We both really wanted that honor back after everything we were put through. Upon hearing from several legal advisors aside from our great legal team, we were told that I would be hurting myself by speaking out. As you saw in this chapter, though, things got worse by keeping quiet because no one could help me. I should have walked out of those dinners and "celebrations" once I was introduced as a "co-valedictorian." While I may have lost the respect of the smartest people in Orange County at the valedictorian dinners, at least the truth would have gotten out. I take full responsibility for listening to bad legal advice and realize I should have been more vocal, but I know I did the best that I could with the available knowledge at the time.

This chapter, for me, was not about my valedictorian title. It wasn't even about me. It was about what happened following my father's role in the investigation and the scars it left on my family. At the end of that week, my family and I all came together and agreed there could be another May 20 between then and the day of my high school graduation (which would not be held for another month). While there were only three weeks left in my high school career, any of those days could easily become another powder keg. These conversations took place as a growing number of teachers and concerned parents privately encouraged my family to file a lawsuit and put an end to this. Newburgh has been around for over 220 years, which is about just as old as the country. For as long as NFA has handed out valedictorian titles, there has never been a story like this with so much documentation. It was obvious that what happened to me was coming thanks to Realist. Realist's anger stunned my father's supporters, and the events that took place following his/her post were simply too much for them. Perhaps you, the reader, felt the same way. People recognized that we could not just move on from this, despite my accomplishments, because of the mental strain this experience put on my family . Therefore, reacting appropriately to such a week was an emergency of the highest magnitude because we weren't sure who else in the community would get hurt. After looking at all of the evidence we had at our disposal, we agreed that a lawsuit would be our best course of action.

Joey Johns May 20th text messages between the reporter and my father. Read from left to right, top down.

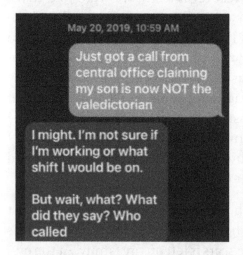
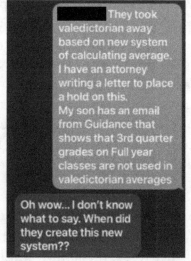

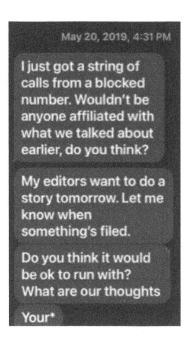

Over the weekend

Good story for you now

May 20, 2019, 4:31 PM

I just got a string of calls from a blocked number. Wouldn't be anyone affiliated with what we talked about earlier, do you think?

My editors want to do a story tomorrow. Let me know when something's filed.

Do you think it would be ok to run with? What are our thoughts

Your*

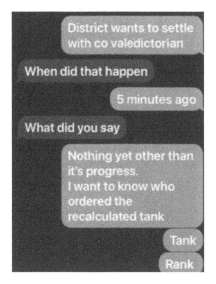

District wants to settle with co valedictorian

When did that happen

5 minutes ago

What did you say

Nothing yet other than it's progress.
I want to know who ordered the recalculated tank

Tank

Rank

But he shouldn't have to share

Should he?

I mean everything's ultimately up to you

Don't let me influence anything ever

No. He should not
It's up to my son and my family

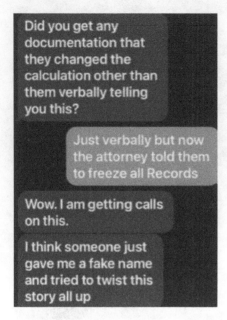

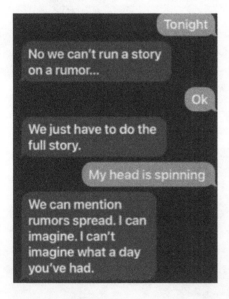

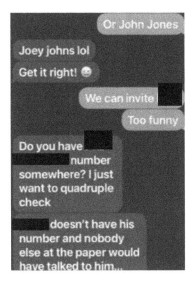

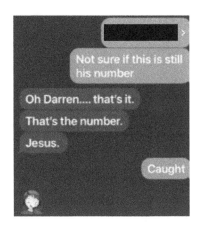

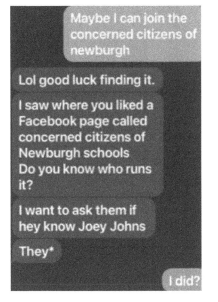

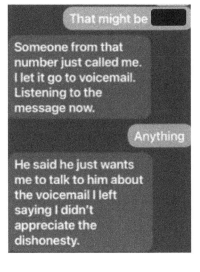

Not calling back until I'm back at work tomorrow, per editors direction. And I'll probably call him with ▮▮▮▮ there for back up.

May 21st text messages regarding Joey Johns.

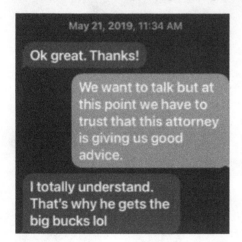

May 21, 2019, 11:34 AM

Ok great. Thanks!

We want to talk but at this point we have to trust that this attorney is giving us good advice.

I totally understand. That's why he gets the big bucks lol

Is that letter saying Matthew is the valedictorian on May 13 filed with the suit? My editors want to use it since I showed it to them yesterday to pitch the story. It's the only thing we have with official word from the school saying he was given the honor. The district didn't put out anything official on the website.

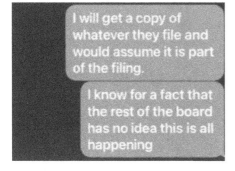

I will get a copy of whatever they file and would assume it is part of the filing.

I know for a fact that the rest of the board has no idea this is all happening

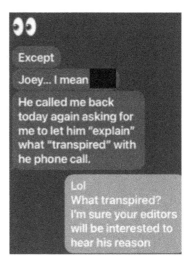

👀

Except

Joey... I mean ▇

He called me back today again asking for me to let him "explain" what "transpired" with he phone call.

Lol
What transpired?
I'm sure your editors will be interested to hear his reason

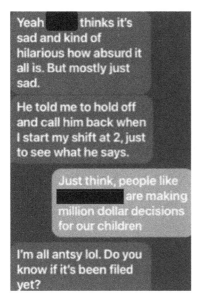

Yeah ▇ thinks it's sad and kind of hilarious how absurd it all is. But mostly just sad.

He told me to hold off and call him back when I start my shift at 2, just to see what he says.

Just think, people like ▇ are making million dollar decisions for our children

I'm all antsy lol. Do you know if it's been filed yet?

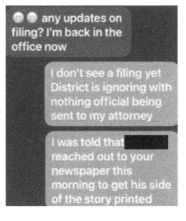

👀👀 any updates on filing? I'm back in the office now

I don't see a filing yet District is ignoring with nothing official being sent to my attorney

I was told that ▇ reached out to your newspaper this morning to get his side of the story printed

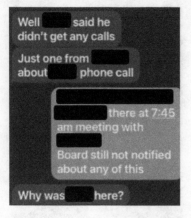

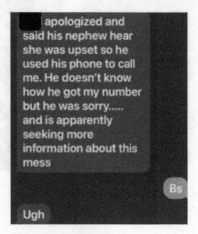

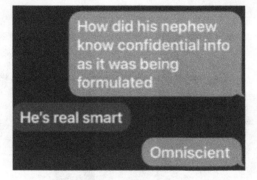

CHAPTER ENDNOTES

1   All text messages can be viewed in the Google Drive. https://drive.google.com/drive/u/2/folders/1kn1XR_oG9mTYuWx-3B_1RDogXrjyNjWqF

2   Emails can be found in Google Drive.

3   Katelyn Cordero, "Retired teacher: school rules not enforced," *Times Hudson Valley*, April 17, 2019, https://www.timeshudsonvalley.com/stories/retired-teacher-school-rules-not-enforced,5529

4   See Google Drive. Social media post also available at https://www.facebook.com/recordonline/posts/10156442245516298

5   See Google Drive.

6   Ibid

7   Ibid

8   Ibid

9   Ibid

10   Ibid

11   Ibid

12   Ibid

13   Ibid

14   Ibid

15   Ibid

16   "Newburgh Free Academy Names Valedictorian and Salutatorian," Newburgh Enlarged City School District, May 22, 2019, https://www.newburghschools.org/nfa-news.php?storynum=1523

17   "P-TECH Around the World," https://www.ptech.org/around-the-world/

18   See Joey Johns texts in the Google Drive

19   Lana Bellamy, "Newburgh school board member files complaint with state over son's co-valedictorian status," *Times Herald-Record*, June 10, 2019, https://www.recordonline.com/story/news/2019/06/11/son-s-co-valedictorian-status/4883810007/

8
SEARCHING FOR ANSWERS
MAY 28, 2019 – JUNE 25, 2019

I hear many stories about many people, but to this day, I have heard of only one or two people who went through similar experiences as me. As the district officials continued to use the "co-valedictorian" title, I planned out my first lawsuit as a seventeen-year-old high school senior. I planned to take this case to as many high-level courts as I could, including the Supreme Court, until I got my valedictorian title back. According to the attorney, I couldn't take my case there right away. New York State law mandated that we direct these types of cases to the NYSED's Commissioner of Education first before proceeding to the upper courts.

School taught me a lot of lessons, yet none of them covered how to win a court case. Within the first two days of my demotion, though, I already had a thirteen-page document written. Sadly, this paperwork was not even close to done. Similar to how NECSD spent a whole weekend coming up with a new policy, my family and I spent all weekend drafting our lawsuit. Much of my weekend involved gathering anything I could find about anyone targeting me with the title, while the others on the legal team researched common law to ensure our case was not thrown out for procedural missteps. It only took a few hours for the evidence file to go from Exhibit A to Exhibit L. Each exhibit featured two or three different pictures, social media posts, text messages, and emails. When you factored in the rest of my team's work, it lengthened the document to forty-eight pages.[1] Newburgh's lead newspaper called it a ten-page complaint, and the social media posts from the source in the previous chapter confirm this statement negatively impacted how people viewed the strength of my lawsuit.[2]

As you can imagine, making a forty-eight page document was no easy task. We needed to file the case very carefully because my attorneys had to meet the burden of proof requested by the Commissioner. According to the New York State Education Department's website, it says that we "must show through documentary evidence, pleadings that are verified (sworn to as correct and accurate), and affidavits that [I] have been directly injured by the district's action. [I] must show that the respondent (usually the school district) either (1) violated a statute or regulation; or (2) acted arbitrarily and capriciously."[3] Our lawyers encouraged my family not to file until we had all of the evidence to prove that the district acted arbitrarily. We needed the guidance counselor's email, we needed statements from the reporters, and we needed proof of retaliatory nature. All of that came together, and through their professional judgment as one of the few law firms in the state to successfully win a case against the Newburgh school district, our attorneys felt now was the time to file. These valedictorian lawsuits are typically not brought to the NYSED until a month after the honor is revoked. Regardless, this case moved with extraordinary speed. The district took away my title on May 20, 2019. My attorneys finalized the forty-eight-page document on May 28. I never expected to send out a lawsuit in that kind of time frame, so I was pleased with the level of cooperation. Frankly, it doesn't happen too often in Newburgh. There was plenty of back-and-forth communication to verify we had everything we needed aside from fact-checking and proofreading. Based on what we read, previous valedictorians who appealed to the Commissioner were denied their titles because the other students involved were not handed the court documents. Anyone that could be injured by a ruling needed to be given our legal paperwork. We verified with our attorneys through text messages that the other co-valedictorian and new salutatorian received the court documents before giving approval to officially send them to the NYSED.

Although it had only been eight days since the district named me co-valedictorian, the district and the parents of the other students already received a lawsuit on their desks. When my dad appeared at the next board meeting, the district's clerk walked into an adjacent room with a large stack of papers in his hand. Twenty minutes later, my dad said he stormed out. Once he noticed my dad, my father told me he had this horrified look on his face aimed directly at him as if the clerk couldn't believe what we were demanding. The administration had five days to explain everything that happened in the previous week to the Commissioner, which was as little time as my legal team and I had. We were also demanding a "stay request," which would temporarily force the district to name me as the sole valedictorian until this case received an actual ruling from her.

The case followed me through the last four remaining Newburgh Free Academy senior celebrations: another valedictorian dinner, the senior scholarship award night, another dinner for student athletes, and the annual senior prom. The NECSD called me the "co-valedictorian" at each of them. When I was not in public, it became routine to find me bunkered down in my parents' basement preparing filings about the valedictorian dispute. I couldn't even leave my house anymore.

My lawyers recommended that I see a clinical psychologist trained in adjustment disorder, PTSD, depression, and anxiety. I searched through at least a hundred online "About Me" biographies of therapists on the Internet before finding someone that I felt comfortable meeting with about my problems. He gave me a very fast response like the attorneys. My first therapy session ever would take place in the middle of the afternoon.

I was supposed to meet him in a building overlooking a nearby highway, but it was divided up into three separate living spaces that had been transformed by the local businesses and organizations occupying them over the years. Of the three entrances, I was supposed to enter through a red door on the far-left side of the building. The interior of the building had an oscillating tower fan, as well as an air conditioner next to a row of chairs on my right. It was dark enough where one could find it just suitable enough for reading. There was chatter ahead behind another closed door in the hallway.

After taking some time to skim through some of the books and science magazines in the waiting lounge, a door by the hallway opened. The therapist and his patient walked out.

"Alright. You can come in," said the psychologist.

I entered another air-conditioned room. This one was just as cool as the last.

"You want water, juice, soda?" he asked.

"No thanks," I answered.

He gestured for me to sit on his couch while he grabbed his note-pad on the table next to a chair across from the couch. The therapist kept all of the items he needed for a session in this room, even some board games and stuffed animals, which had names for his young-er patients.

"Matthew, did you have any dreams last night?"

I looked back up at him.

"I... think I did."

It's just I couldn't remember many of the details in my dreams any-more. The only complete dreams that I remembered had to be at least from six years prior. In my most vivid one, I stood alone on a black platform in the middle of a shadowy black citadel. Empty pris-on gates and a green oozing substance surrounded me. Yellow wisps of electricity crackled in iron cages above the platforms. This place had likely been abandoned years earlier, given its design. I sought to escape this prison. The only way to escape would have been to jump across a series of black platforms until I reached the very last one. It was the only thing I could do, so I started moving. Platform by plat-form, I made my way across them while keeping my focus on the empty cells, the wisps, the platforms, and the bubbling substance. I was almost at the end, yet my overconfidence got to me. I jumped too soon, and thus, I fell into the substance. Although the green liquid was painless, I gave out a scream that echoed through the rest of the prison. Shadow enveloped me as the dream transitioned to focus on other aspects of the jail, none of which I remember entirely, and that was it. I woke up to find myself not in confinement, but rather in the comfort of my own home.

I told the psychologist more about these unusual dreams to get a better understanding of what I was going through. During one dream, I looked for desperately needed medical supplies on an island surrounded by purple rock and sea. In another, I encountered a shooter in Newburgh, only to find myself running away from him in New York City. It was always interesting to hear the therapist's interpretation since he believed the dreams were symbolic of my ongoing struggles and my fight against injustice. Jumping across the platforms may have reflected my autonomy and fighting spirit. His theory had merit. This dream took place during a very stressful school year. Up until May 2019, that school year made up a majority of the most stressful experiences in my life. My dreams have never been the same ever since. What I saw in my sleep was mostly darkness. These highly complex scenes that I could break down transformed into random thoughts that I immediately forgot when I woke up. I became more focused on the present and what was going on at the high school.

My psychologist has worked in his field for a very long time. Nonetheless, he told me that he has not heard about the types of things that I experienced. The therapist said to me he agreed that something wasn't right. As I finished talking with him and exited the room, he wanted to talk separately with my parents. They told him about the sleepless nights we all had preparing court filings and how our attorney's directives were being ignored. Sometimes, we were up until one in the morning doing work. Filing a lawsuit takes a lot of energy, and having to relive those experiences by writing and talking about them made my family's situation worse. To this day, those experiences are what I remember most about my last few weeks of high school.

One day while I was near the therapist's office, one of the reporters who interviewed me at my college graduation texted me a surprise. Attached to her message were photos of the graduation. The front page of her newspaper talked about the P-TECH graduation.

"In today's paper! Made the cover!"

"Wow! This is great. Thanks for the great news!"

"Glad you like it."

"I have an update on the valedictorian case as well!" My mind wouldn't stop thinking about it. *"I'm hearing that people can FOIL the filing from the district now too. There's a [BOE] policy committee meeting later today. Perhaps you can get it then? Talk with the [NECSD] District Clerk."*

"Will let you know. Another reporter at the paper might be taking this story, as I have limited time until the end of the school year. Is that ok?"

"Ok."

FOIL/FOIA are acronyms in New York State that stand for the Freedom of Information Law. It allows anyone in the world to access New York court and government documents, including those pertaining to my case, within a matter of days. If you, the reader, want to access any of my court records that aren't already in the Google Drive, you can just ask the NECSD's district clerk for them through his email. His email can be found on the district's website.

My family gave court documents to the superintendent, the assistant superintendent, the NFA North/Main/P-TECH principals, my guidance counselor, a district media liaison at my college graduation, the person accused of being Joey Johns, and a few other miscellaneous administrators so they could respond to our inquiries. Out of the twelve administrators, only the superintendent and the assistant superintendent responded to the filing. This meant that all of the claims my family made about the other district officials have to legally be assumed to be true. According to the NYSED's website, "If a respondent fails to answer, the statements in the petition (my filing) are deemed to be true."[4] Based on the responses we received, the administration made mistakes.[5] Citing policies and an email that was sent to the assistant superintendent on the day before I received my valedictorian title, the district suddenly denied that they made a new policy over the weekend by saying their formula for class rank dates back to 1982 and had always incorporated third-quarter grades. The email mentions a "3rd quarter rank," though it is unclear what that means (it could be interpreted as including or excluding grades up to third quarter). A software error supposedly prevented my NFA Main courses from appearing on my academic records before the recalculation. Lower level employees - particularly the principals - were blamed for handing me the valedictorian letter and "misinformation." I supposedly should have never received a party at the high schools because none of my grades from NFA Main were ever transferred to NFA North. When the administration hand-calculated my GPA over the weekend, I was 0.04 points below my opponent.

What this dispute ultimately comes down to, aside from Joey John's phone call and Realist's social media post, was their math. The district's paperwork claimed that they recalculated my GPA at the requests of both the salutatorian's parents and the second co-valedictorian's parents, but the NECSD never offered any evidence to support this claim. While the students supposedly had their requests granted, the district never granted my attorney's requests to let me see how my GPA was recalculated. Learning about the district's new class rank formula is something I am entitled to know as a New York high school student. There is a law called the Family Educational Rights and Privacy Act (FERPA) that gives me the right to obtain this information. FERPA was the reason why my guidance counselor had to inform me about the district's original class-rank policy. According to the district's student records policy, "Pursuant to FERPA, it shall be the policy of this school district to permit parents/guardians and eligible students to inspect and review any and all official records, files and data directly related to that student, including all materials that are incorporated into each student's cumulative record folder."[6]

When the district refused to give me their math, I suspected fraud. Because the DA's investigation found they are capable of manipulating attendance records, their past wrongdoings suggest there is nothing stopping them from lowering my grades and naming me a co-valedictorian based on altered information. To confirm my suspicions, I needed my transcript. The document had all of my recent grades.

Back at Main Campus, second period ended. I walked through the hallway and into the Guidance Office before leaving school for the day. A phone rang. Two students were in front of me in the line. In case anything happened, I recorded everything that was said using my cell phone.

"Hello, I'll call you back later." The woman in the office hung up the phone. She talked with two students briefly.

"Ok. You're first. You're staying with me. You are also staying with me."

She then looked at me.

"You?"

"I just wanted to request if I can get my transcript printed out fast."

"Sure."

A minute went by and a paper came out of the printer. It was the transcript.

"Matt, do you want it in an envelope?"

"I'll be ok."

The line was much longer now. I must have come at the right time. Back home, I compared this June transcript I received from Main to a February transcript that I received from NFA North. Although the district claims a software error prevented my courses taken at NFA Main from appearing on my records at North, both the February and the June transcript that I received contain a final GPA in my government course. Since both of the transcripts contain my grades from NFA Main, my findings completely contradict the district's claims. In addition to my government course appearing on the transcripts, my English course also appeared on various report cards that I received from my guidance counselor at North. Here are two such report cards that I received on November 21, 2018 and February 8, 2019 respectively, several months before the recalculation actually occurred (Exhibit 1).

Attendance Summary:

Terms:	Q1		Q2		Q3		Q4		Total	
Course	Absent	Tardy	Absent	Tardy	Absent	Tardy	Absent	Tardy	Absent	Tardy
140 AP GOVERNMENT US	1	0	0	0	0	0	0	0	1	0
019 ENGLISH 12R	1	1	0	0	0	0	0	0	1	1

Attendance Summary:

Terms:	Q1		Q2		Q3		Q4		Total	
Course	Absent	Tardy	Absent	Tardy	Absent	Tardy	Absent	Tardy	Absent	Tardy
140 AP GOVERNMENT US	1	0	1	0	0	0	0	0	2	0
137 AP MACROECONOMICS	0	0	0	0	2	0	0	0	2	0
019 ENGLISH 12R	1	1	1	0	1	0	0	0	3	1

Exhibit 1 – Report cards forwarded to me by the guidance counselor.

With that being said, there is no software error which could have forced the district to recalculate anything. Yet, what was more interesting to me is how the district added a gym class from SUNY Orange onto my June transcript without telling the Commissioner and my family. The grade was wrong and actually lowered my GPA. It should have been an A, not an A-. I needed to work with the college to fix that.

In the meantime, my father was studying the Facebook posts about my valedictorian case very carefully. He had recently heard from someone that the district took away valedictorian titles from students as early as 2013, and social media posts confirm the rumor. (Parts of the following social media posts may have been altered to protect the identities of individuals. However, their content still conveys their original meaning.) In response to a newspaper article about this valedictorian situation, someone wrote, "Unfortunately, Newburgh has a habit of 'recalculating' these decisions. A VERY similar situation happened once, but the young lady (the former valedictorian) decided to move on without fighting for her true place in the standings. Shame on the NFA staff."[7] One of the former valedictorian's parents responded to an identical post. The mother wrote, "They did a last minute change also."[8] My father took screenshots of these posts within hours of their creation. The parent never elaborated on how her daughter was demoted from valedictorian. If she had any evidence for her claims, it would be clear that the district hasn't been using the same class rank policy since 1982. The only way to verify whether these accusations were true was if my family either talked with the former valedictorian or the parent who responded to the story on social media. My father really wanted to be the one who talked with them. Through more research, he contacted one of the former valedictorian's parents while I was at school. At first, he was greeted by an automated message. Once he asked to speak with the parent, he was transferred to her line. Talking with her was an opportunity he could not pass up, so he got his audio recorder ready for his own recollection. (All of the parties [including the parent] had the chance to respond to what my father learned as you will see. The district was also given this audio recording for reasons you'll see later in the book, allowing them to do a follow-up investigation. If you want to review the evidence for yourself, you could make a FOIA request.).

Imagine being the valedictorian of your class for the entire year. Unlike in my case, you shared the news with the entire school. Everyone knew. Your friends would see you in the cafeteria at the lunch table and always say, "Oh! There's our valedictorian!" People would always come to you for help with homework because they knew you were the smartest kid in the school district. Next thing you know, you only had four weeks left of high school. You were expected to give a graduation speech. As the district finalized the class ranking, other district employees simultaneously released the results on the school district website. You read them for yourself, and you learned you were no longer the valedictorian. You became the salutatorian. The person who was ranked #3 in the class somehow became the new class valedictorian.

Immediately, you called up your mother. She was just as surprised as you. "Whaat?" she reacted. "You and the former salutatorian were ranked one and two, and the new valedictorian was originally ranked number three. How did that happen?!" As the parent, she reached out to the school's guidance counselors who also expected you to become the valedictorian. They were almost as surprised as you and recommended that your mother follow her gut instinct, which was to contact the district's top administrators. They told your mother exactly what they told my father: we recalculated grades based on a new policy that factored in high school courses taken in eighth grade. However, the courses only applied to your GPA if you took them in Newburgh. As an eighth grader, you didn't attend a Newburgh school. You attended a private school. The administration allegedly told your mother that the high school courses you aced back then don't count in your individual class rank calculation anymore because they were weighted differently. This caused your GPA to drop, and since the new valedictorian was enrolled at the NECSD in eighth grade, the new valedictorian's overall GPA was now ahead of yours by a mere one-tenth of a point.

How would you feel if you learned that your valedictorian title, which you worked four years for, was suddenly stripped from you after a group of people came together at the last minute and randomly decided to calculate class rank based on a brand new policy? There is no justification for this. Nonetheless, that's the exact story my father heard over the phone! During the school year that this valedictorian was a senior, my father served on the BOE's Policy Committee. Any such class rank policy changes would have to go through that committee. My father replied in amazement. "That is so odd. I don't even remember that coming up and I was on that committee!" Luckily, my father rediscovered the policy during the interview. In the next figure, you can see that this policy was introduced to the BOE on May 9. At the very bottom of the figure, the policy matches up with what the parent told my father because it says, "Honors classes taken prior to 9th grade will be included." These courses were even weighted differently from standard high school courses, as the policy shows students would receive a GPA bonus of 3%. For example, a student who normally earns a 100 over-all GPA in an honors course would now receive a 103. This explains how the new valedictorian was able to surpass the original valedictorian and salutatorian.

Agenda Item Details

Meeting	May 09, ▮▮▮ - Policy Committee
Category	1. Policy Agenda Items
Subject	1.04 Class Rank and Weighting of Grades
Type	Discussion

The weighting of grades will occur for the purpose of establishing senior class rank only. The purpose of weighting is to encourage students to undertake coursework of a more challenging nature.

High school courses carrying credit will be weighted according to the following:

Honors Courses	1.03
College Credit Courses	1.08
Advanced Placement Courses	1.10

Honors classes taken prior to 9th grade will be included.

1.04 Class Rank and Weighting of Grades

The administration would like a policy on class rank and the weighting of grades that is clear and concise.

The committee inquired if this policy will be for senior class rank only and not for report cards? Will reports cards reflect grades over 100? data to compare. What about AP classes that give you college credit, would those grades be weighted?

The committee requested for the June committee meeting the answers to the questions posed be ready for discussion.

If you cannot read the text off of these images, please look at the Google Drive.

Every policy committee hearing contains a meeting summary of what was discussed. My father's initial reaction to seeing this policy was that he thought the NECSD wanted to change the way things were graded in the future, not the present. Other BOE members felt the same way. Attached to the policy were various meeting notes. The figure (1.04 Class Rank) offers an excerpt of the comments. I couldn't fit all of the comments here due to spacing concerns, yet you can see that all three BOE members concluded the new class rank policy needed to be more concise. They would meet again in June to discuss everything further, but the NECSD administration didn't have until June to name a valedictorian. Class valedictorian is named in May every year, so it appears that the administration used an unapproved policy to arbitrarily recalculate class rank for the entire senior class without the BOE's knowledge! All school district policies must be approved by the BOE before they are implemented, making any prior usage of the policy illegal. As word spread about the new recalculation, this valedictorian was honored with the salutatorian title at every senior "celebration." People came up to the parent with the words, "Your daughter got robbed. I can't believe they did that to her." So many people approached the parent that she even started emailing district administrators about the concerns of her colleagues. This parent, thankfully, voluntarily chose to forward these emails to my father. As a result, we can present them in this book (Exhibit 2). On June 5, she emailed an administrator with several questions on her mind.

> "I was told to contact you with a question that has been bothering me. There are several stories about the last-minute change in Valedictorian/Salutatorian rank, and I was hoping to get some clarity. My daughter had held the Valedictorian spot literally until the day the grades were finalized. For my own peace of mind, I am wondering exactly what happened."

The administrator never answered, so she wrote back eight days later.

> "I had called last week with a few questions that I just wanted answered. I realize the end of the year is hectic, so when you get a chance can you email me the answers please. [I] wanted to know exactly when the recalculation was done. And you had mentioned that this recalculation was done based on a new procedure to make the process more even across the board for the students? This was a new procedure just done for this senior class and will be the method used going forward? Or will the new method be implemented next year going forward?"

She never received a response, but it was abundantly clear that what happened to me took place before.

Fwd: Class Rank Question
1 message

█████████████████████████████████   Thu, Jun 13, 2019 at 8:36 AM

To: ████████████████████

---------- Forwarded message ----------
From: █████████████████████████████
Date:
Subject: Re: Class Rank Question
To: █████████████████████ @necsd.net>

Good Morning

I had called last week with a few questions that my husband had that I just wanted to make sure that I was answering him correctly.
I realize end of year is hectic, so when you get a chance can you email me the answers please.

He wanted to know exactly when the recalculation was done.
And you had mentioned that this recalculation was done based on a new procedure to make the process more even across the board for the students? This was a new procedure just done for this senior class and will be the method used going forward? Or will the new method be implemented next year going forward?

Thank you for your time.

On ███ wrote:
Good Morning,

My daughter ████████████ is the NFA Class of ████ Salutatorian.
I was told to contact you with a question that has been bothering me.
There are several stories about the last minute change in Valedictorian/Salutatorian rank, and I was hoping to get some clarity.
My daughter had held the Valedictorian spot literally until the day the grades were finalized.
For my own peace of mind, I am wondering exactly what happened.

I would appreciate if you could reach out to me via email or phone at your earliest convenience.

Thank you in advance for your time.

██████████████

Exhibit 2 -- Emails forwarded to my father. These were both later submitted to the NYSED.

After the conversation, my dad called my mom. She had just picked me up from school. When he explained everything, we knew that we finally had the smoking gun that should convince the Commissioner to approve the stay request before NFA's graduation. The evidence against the NECSD was now irrefutable. They didn't just take my valedictorian title. They did it to other people too at the last minute! Half an hour later, we were all working at home. While my mother cooked lunch, my father contacted our attorneys and prepared an affidavit for the parent to sign. I took notes from the recorded interview, which my team needed to create a second case filing that would be sent to the Commissioner's office. I've never been filled with so much enthusiasm. Maybe it was true that the district has been calculating class rank using third-quarter grades since 1982, but there are clearly exceptions to when they use this policy because a new class rank formula was used during this school year. Despite what the NECSD claims, this evidence suggests there isn't a definitive class rank policy.

The steps taken to rename the valedictorian of a previous school year were identical to the steps taken against me, yet the NECSD told the Commissioner that they used the same system to determine class rank since 1982. Once again, what we discovered goes against what the district said in its paperwork. This time, we have evidence to prove that the district came up with a new system that included eighth-grade scores, they recalculated class rank at the last minute, the former valedictorian dropped to salutatorian, and other people unfairly lost their ranking because of it. Apparently, the former salutatorian also attends Columbia University. The parent told my father that she started a foundation where she sent off books to kids while she was in high school. As a result of all of these different policies, the true valedictorian and salutatorian may never learn what her actual GPA is. All we know is that, just as in my case, the math was altered.

Eventually, my college gym instructor agreed that the A- should actually be an A. Once the grade was corrected on my college transcript, NFA legally had to update my high school transcript. However, they refused to correct anything because doing so would force them to rename me as the sole valedictorian of my class. This prompted my family to report the NECSD to the Commissioner of Education using our second case filing. It contains the class rank policy which incorporates eight-grade classes, the emails, along with a thorough explanation. Once we submitted that filing, though, many shady things started happening.

Around the time the NECSD got a request for comment from the media about what we learned, my attorney sent an affidavit to the parent so she could sign it. She told my father to keep her updated, so we did. Yet for some odd reason, she never replied. She refused to answer any emails. She never took phone calls from my attorney. It was like she disappeared. How does one go from being very transparent to very quiet in just a few days? It wasn't just her who was quiet. In fact, the district never responded with a comment regarding a story which covered this incident. Every other person in a leadership position who my family gave the evidence to became quiet as well. If someone retaliated against the parent, which is what certain people have done in the past (see "A Call To Action," "Unleash the Kraken," "Shattered"), then my family needed to find out. However, no one was willing to investigate that, and the NYSED was quick to follow up. On the day before my NFA graduation, her office notified my attorney that the NYSED denied the stay request in favor of the NECSD. It was not the final ruling. Still, it does set the precedent for that decision. My dad assumed her office wanted to review more evidence, but I said the NYSED did not need any additional information to hand back my title and help the parent. I told him that there is good reason to believe something big is being hidden in Newburgh beyond the valedictorian dispute. If we were able to show that my valedictorian title and another girl's valedictorian title were taken away in the exact same manner, how many other people has the district done this to? This is a very important question that the NYSED did not express interest in! Of the newspapers who did report on my evidence, many people who commented on Facebook felt the same way and were furious at the NYSED (Exhibit 3).[9] One person posted on social media, "With all the corruption and scandals going on in the district, why isn't the state getting involved in this?" Another added, "This just sucks for the Class of 2019."

Sad....

Like · Reply · 2y

Oh oh

Like · Reply · 2y

Darren is fighting for the most important principle of government: open and consistent application of the rules. This goes far beyond the matter of who is valedictorian.

Like · Reply · 2y

thank you for your comment your comment is right to the point and so true. My problem is why isn't the board doing their job to remove the corruption from the district starting from the top if you have a person that is the superintendent that a...
See more

Like · Reply · 2y · Edited

maybe the board should be looked at.

Like · Reply · 2y

This just sucks for the class of 2019

Like · Reply · 2y

↳ replied · 2 Replies

With all the corruption and Scandals going on in the district why isn't the state getting involved in this.

Like · Reply · 2y

But it leaves a cloud over the top students in the graduating class it affects many students and families and should be a happy time

Like · Reply · 2y

Horrible, what is happening! Disgraceful!

Like · Reply · 2y

Exhibit 3 -- Comments of residents after hearing the news of the second valedictorian. Source: https://www.facebook.com/darren.stridiron.9/ posts/2524727260894508

On the day of the graduation, all of the seniors were expected to attend the rehearsal. The co-valedictorian, salutatorian, and I were supposed to lead the class out of the building to a football field where our diplomas would be handed to us later in the day. Many of the teachers sat by the bleachers surrounding the football field. My dad told me school policy requires them to attend. However, none of the teachers saw me. One of them texted my father, "Is Matthew not going to the graduation?"[10]

The night before, my parents treated me to dessert at my favorite local ice cream shop after hearing the terrible news from the NYSED. I already posted something on social media confirming that I would attend the graduation, but I thought twice. I didn't attend the rehearsal. Instead, I laid in bed as rain poured onto my windowsills. The house was quiet and dead. I wasn't really sad. I was disgusted. The NYSED sided with the NECSD and made this a graduation I will never forget. Teachers were so sickened by all of the recent events inside the NYSED that they didn't even want to attend NFA's graduation, despite it being mandatory for them to do so. One of them texted my father, "First graduation I won't attend. I am so sad that ethics and morals seem to be gone."[11]

While she had already made up her mind, the same decision was not that easy for me because I was supposed to lead my class. I called my grandfather an hour after I got out of bed and told him what happened. I wasn't too sure if I'd attend. I'll never forget the way he said "I don't blame ya" because he really wanted to see one of his grandchildren graduate from high school.

Two hours before the commencement, I read over the speech that I was expected to present before thousands of faculty, students, and parents. It took weeks to finalize the speech with everything else that was happening, but reading the printed copy after adding those last-minute changes proved to me it was time well spent. People were still calling up my father. "Is Matthew attending?" they asked. Within the past hour, I gave him permission to answer with a yes. Similar to the day when the NECSD took my title, I would not let the actions of the NYSED interfere with my duties as a sole valedictorian. Ultimately, I told my grandfather, "If I go, I'm going just for you." I would speak before my class just so he could watch me.

Before I left my house, I stuffed the folded, stapled copy of my script into my jeans as the rest of my family waited outside to take pictures. It wasn't raining anymore. Unlike the SUNY Orange graduation, NFA's celebration was blessed with clear skies. The parking lot at NFA Main was overcrowded when we arrived. Students from both high school campuses were instructed earlier in the morning to gather there half-an-hour before the main procession. My family found a place to park at the school's lower lobby. Hopefully, this would be the last time I'd have to come back here. Everyone who approached me couldn't wait to hear the speech. The people inside the building directed me up a flight of stairs and into a room where the other co-valedictorian and salutatorian were waiting. A teacher in a black graduation outfit and yellow sache soon lined everyone up in the hallway. The other co-valedictorian, salutatorian, and I would lead the class. Similar to the rehearsal, we directed an entire hallway of students out a side door and toward NFA Main's front entrance. Over six hundred graduates were waiting together outside for the cue to proceed into the school's football field. We really couldn't leave where we were standing because that would alter who sits in which seat at the ceremony, but groups of friends were still able to gather in front of photographers for one last picture together. People were also coming up from the football field to congratulate us.

"Matt! Thank goodness I found you. People were saying you weren't going to show up."

I turned to see my middle school technology teacher. She was one of the people who asked me to speak to her classes earlier in the year.

"Almost," I replied.

"Wait. The rumors were true? Why?" asked the teacher. The second co-valedictorian briefly turned around in shock.

"Don't worry. All that matters is that I'm here," I assured her, not knowing how else to answer her.

"Ok... I understand." I could tell she knew what I was thinking.

"Oh!" she remembered. "One last thing. Are we still on for lunch tomorrow?"

"Definitely."

"Alright. Take care, Matthew. Can't wait to hear your graduation speech!"

She came to me at the right time. Not even two minutes later, the graduates marched in a two-by-two fashion along the concrete path to the school's football field. I could already hear the cheers of spectators in the distance and the buzzing of drones outside of the school gates, which we call Academy Field. We entered the football field and walked halfway down it. A cameraman livestreaming the event greeted us.[12] An announcer turned on his microphone near the spectators by the high school and introduced the band. Once they started playing "Pop and Circumstance," the same song as the one at the SUNY Orange graduation, that was our signal to make a right turn along the field's forty-yard line toward the packed bleachers, another right turn to wave to the spectators, and one final right turn toward the center stage where I would present my speech. The second co-valedictorian, salutatorian, and I sat in our three reserved seats on the stage while the rest of the class found their seats on the field. It took about ten minutes for everyone to get seated. The administration and the Board of Education Members were sitting to my left.

When the music ended, the announcer started talking again:

"Ladies and gentlemen. Please be seated. Welcoming you this evening: our co-principals!"

Since the majority of students attended NFA Main, their principal spoke first. By the time they both finished, the graduates were already throwing beach balls around the field. Like SUNY, it is a tradition at Newburgh Free Academy, but it ended once the salutatorian gave her speech. I was next.

"Newburgh Free Academy co-valedictorian: Matthew Stridiron!" the announcer shouted.

The public was going to hear my speech for the first time. I insisted on working on it alone because I didn't want anyone to hear the address before the graduation. There was already a copy of my speech enclosed in a plastic sheath on the podium, but it lacked the latest revisions. That was when I took the updated speech out of my jeans. I stepped up to the podium and looked at the crowd sitting before me.

"Congratulations, Class of 2019! We made it!" I announced. Cheers soon followed.

Graduation symbolizes a myriad of great things. With a diploma to be in your hands, you proved that Newburgh is one strong community whose members stand up for what they believe in. You put your skills and character to the test, and you should all be extremely proud of your success.

This community is what I want to talk about. There's a famous saying that states, 'It takes a village to raise a child.' Communities play an important part in influencing our life stories. They mold the memories we make, the challenges we overcome, and the ideas we attain. If one finds his or her sense of belonging, that individual will leave a positive footprint on the world.

However, communities don't just sprout up out of nowhere. They require bonds as well as input, which in this case are the local residents' ideas, in order to hold them together. When combined, they can change a community.

But these elements are dying in the United States. While there are many opportunities to volunteer, it is becoming more challenging to find them, especially for those who lack social connections.

For five years, I was in this same boat. It was hard for me to figure out what to do because I was stuck in a closed environment where I was silenced. And the drama made me unable to work on projects that intended to bring Newburgh together.

Now, my intent is not to complain here on stage. In fact, I don't regret a day in my life. The good days gave me joy, and the bad ones merely gave me a new way of thinking.

Ideally, people work with one another, but instead, I learned that not everyone has a say. Some individuals want to interact with people, but they are bullied. Others are completely ignored, making them unaware of the opportunities surrounding them.

Has this group of people always been marginalized? If so, this is dangerous. When we exclude people, we're not cultivating a community. Instead, we are killing it. When one community falls, others decline as well.

But there is a way that we can give these people a say. In the last two years, I learned that you can never limit yourself to the opportunities that a community has to offer, so I took as many of them as I could. It was important to forge connections with the people that I met.

When I did this, I transitioned from a life of many problems into one where I was free to pursue whatever I wanted. People offered me ways of viewing things that I haven't considered. We all have good ideas about how to improve the area. It's just that we have different ways of expressing the same message.

You know. Graduation is a time to give thanks, so I'd like to give a shoutout to these people. And feel free to clap for them.

First and foremost, my friends from NFA Main. If it weren't for you giving me determination in the first semester, I know for a fact that I wouldn't be up here.

And my friends from North and Middletown (a nearby town). You offered me the chance to gain skills that I can use beyond Academy Field.

And how could I give a graduation speech without mentioning my family? I am so happy to be a Stridiron. People know our determined spirits enable us to keep on fighting towards what we set our minds out to do.

Lastly, my friends from outside Orange County. You're the people who extended my support system farther than I would have ever imagined.

Class of 2019, none of you are cogs in a machine. Each of you are your own person, with a story to tell and lessons to share. Your input is valued, so pursue your dreams by becoming a part of this community.

And of course. Always stay true to yourself, and always fight for what is good. There will always be groups that support good. It is just a matter of finding and working with them. As H. Jackson Brown Jr. once said, 'Throw off the bowlines. Sail away from the safe harbor. Catch the trade winds in your sails. Explore. Dream. Discover.'

Class of 2019. Thank you once again. Congratulations, God bless you, and good night!

The crowd loved it. In almost an instant, the beach balls were back up in the air, and you could hear whistling from the back of the crowd too. The ceremony had two more speeches, one from the other co-valedictorian and the other from the superintendent.

At the end of the superintendent's speech, he declared, "As the Superintendent of Schools, in accordance with the authority granted to me by the New York State Board of Regents, I hereby certify that these candidates have qualified for a New York State high school diploma. I, therefore, authorize members of our Board of Education to present the high school diplomas at this time."

Every person in the field, the bleachers, and behind the school gates cheered when he sat down. The NFA Main principal approached the two students and I to redirect us from the stage to join others in the seats on the field. School security moved the podium away and replaced it with a table of certificate holders for our diplomas at the center of the stage. After just making our way to our new chairs, the second co-valedictorian, salutatorian, and I now had to lead the front row of graduates to receive our diplomas. When my name was called, I walked up the stage again and was greeted by my dad. As a Board of Education member, he could hand me my diploma. We shook hands and hugged, something we anticipated to do on this platform for years (just without all of the drama leading up to it). A photographer greeted me below with my eleventh-grade history teacher, who wished me the best of luck moving forward. For the next hour and a half, it was all about the photos and the awards.

When the ceremony came to a close, the announcer came back on. He stated, "Ladies and gentlemen. As our final graduates make their way back to their seats, for the one-hundred and fifty-fourth year in a row, we are proud to present to you the Newburgh Free Academy Class of 2019!"

The school band started playing "The Gladiator," by John Philip Sousa. Everyone in the field gathered at its center with the beach balls, hugging and walking out the same way we came in. Our path was surrounded by teachers and relatives who offered us one final goodbye. "Go change the world," my twelfth-grade English teacher told me. When I reached the gates of Academy Field, I officially did it. I completed high school. Balloons covered the road while families reunited with their children on the street. Traffic along nearby roads had been closed down just for this occasion. The noise we made could be heard a block away. As security started cleaning up the center stage and everything around it, the music died down. Graduates left. I spent up to half-an-hour looking for anyone I knew, and although I did find some of them, eventually I didn't recognize anyone. I left with my family to celebrate with dinner at a local restaurant shortly afterwards.

I graduated with an Honors Regents Diploma in Mathematics. Every time I look back at my high school career, I always acknowledge the good parts. I would definitely agree that my strongest moment in high school took place at the graduation. Although my family faced immeasurable retaliation, I showed up to this event and fulfilled my duties as a sole valedictorian. Just like on the day where the NECSD took my title, I would not let the actions of these administrators deter me from delivering my graduation speech. I know for a fact that many other valedictorians would have stayed home.

Many people in Newburgh believe that the NYSED is on board with remedying Newburgh's failure to handle attendance issues. After this incident, I began to question that notion. For years, the NYSED was contacted by concerned teachers who provided evidence that data was being altered. The department never responded to them. It only publicly condemned the district after the grand jury's report made headlines.

This valedictorian dispute was a crisis in the making. It's amazing how I didn't see any of the warning signs sooner. Upon talking with an individual about how the NYSED denied my stay request, I sought to determine whether the NYSED is even qualified to handle cases involving their own public school districts. The person who I talked to works in a legal profession and - to my knowledge - wanted to know more about this. The practice of hiring attorneys, preparing legal documents, holding hearings, and receiving opinions is something you would expect to find in a courtroom, not the state education department. Its job is to oversee public education, and yet somehow, New York gave its NYSED Commissioner the powers of a judge to handle legal disputes. I found this to be extremely unusual. While the Commissioner may not know the superintendent personally, she is required to work with him on a professional level. At one point the superintendent apparently wanted one of his plans to be approved by the NYSED. The Commissioner approved it, as part of her job duty, and wrote back to him using glowing terms. In this letter made available to the public, she said things such as, "Congratulations." and "Thank you again for your hard work." Most importantly, she stated, "The New York State Education Department and I look forward to continuing our work together, with the goal of ensuring that every school has world-class educators in the classroom [...]" These phrases demonstrate that, going into my valedictorian dispute, the NYSED "look[ed] forward" to continue working with the superintendent because the department believed his plans could bring "world-class educators" into the classroom.[13]

You can find several other instances of the Commissioner professionally interacting with the superintendent on the Internet, including the NECSD's own Twitter page where the superintendent stood by the Commissioner for a picture.[14] Judges who preside in courtrooms do not have these types of encounters. While the Commissioner was simply performing her duty as an education official by meeting with the superintendent, this obviously raises credibility concerns of a state education department ruling on cases involving their own school districts. It does make sense for the Commissioner to want to get to know Newburgh's superintendent because they work within the same educational field, yet no Commissioner should be tasked with offering a legal opinion regarding the districts that they work with. If there's one thing that comes out of this book, my hope is that lawmakers revise their laws to make sure all education-related matters are delivered to actual courts as opposed to their state education departments. The NYSED is an educational institution whose goal is to teach students, not to serve as a judicial system.

My case isn't a difficult one to win. Despite the NYSED's opinion, I believe my family did meet the NYSED's burden of proof by showing there were questionable things going on within the recalculation. As of the time of this book's publication, the NECSD has yet to correct my final GPA after learning of the error in my SUNY Orange gym class. They could go back into my records right now and update my final GPA!

In the words of someone who read about my dispute, "Darren (my dad) is fighting for the most important principle of government: open and consistent application of the rules. This goes far beyond the matter of who is valedictorian." Had the district and the NYSED demonstrated fairness from the very beginning, there is a possibility that I would have accepted the verdict. There is no doubt the second co-valedictorian, the salutatorian, and I are smart people going to great schools. This has nothing to do with the kids. This dispute is about how my father faced backlash, following the DA's investigation. Whether you are a student athlete, a "regular" high school student, or a valedictorian, your life can be impacted in some form just by having someone alter your GPA. Changing a GPA is so easy to do, and many people I know tell me that I proved my case. At the end of the day, people who know the truth will speak the truth. A week following my graduation, my sixth-grade technology teacher sent me a package with NFA's commencement booklet. It outlined all of the events that took place during the ceremony, as well as the names of the co-valedictorians. She crossed out the "co-" and scribbled out the "s." In its place, she underlined "valedictorian" and added, "Matt, I'm so proud!"

CHAPTER ENDNOTES

1   Court documents can be found in the Google Drive

2   Lana Bellamy, "Newburgh school board member files complaint
     with state over son's co-valedictorian status," *Times Herald-Re-
     cord*, June 10, 2019, https://www.recordonline.com/story/
     news/2019/06/11/son-s-co-valedictorian-status/4883810007/

3   "Frequently Asked Questions Concerning Appeals to the Com-
     missioner of Education," New York State Education Depart-
     ment, http://www.counsel.nysed.gov/appeals/faqs

4   Ibid

5   See Google Drive

6   Ibid

7   Ibid

8   Ibid

9   "No State Ed valedictorian decision with NFA graduation in three
     days," Mid-Hudson News, June 24, 2019, https://midhudson-
     news.com/2019/06/24/no-state-ed-valedictorian-decision-with-
     nfa-graduation-in-three-days/

10   See Google Drive

11   Ibid

12   Sagadahoc, "Newburgh High School Graduation 2019," June
     28, 2019, Youtube video, 1:31:50, https://www.youtube.com/
     watch?v=eNw2LyQnHYU

13   New York State Education Department, Letter to the NECSD
     Superintendent, http://www.nysed.gov/common/nysed/files/
     newburgh-appr-plan-112316.pdf

14   Twitter post, https://twitter.com/newburghschools/sta-
     tus/740194778890022912

ARC THREE

9
LOOKING UP TO FAMILY
SUMMER 2019

Not even two days after my graduation, I took a four-day trip to Texas. When I returned home, a reporter who covered OCCC's graduation wanted to run a story about my high school career and suggested we meet at a local coffee shop. The clock hit noon when I arrived at the building. A saxophone played in the background before the music transitioned to a Country-themed song. A large blackboard near condiments and coffee machines on a back counter listed out all of their breakfast and lunch specials in chalk. After I got my order, I grabbed a nearby newspaper and sat at one of the wooden tables facing the shop's front windows. When I least expected it, a teacher I knew stopped by me. "Congratulations," he said, probably for graduating. "And good luck!"

Soon, the reporter came. Due to the constant whirring of the coffee machines, we moved outside to a table next to the store. We talked a bit about our Fourth of July weekend plans before diving into the main issues. She wrote down everything I said as fast as she could during the hour that we talked. When I read the report one week later, its optimistic language made me happy for the first time in a while. Despite the mountain of praise I received, the events of May and June always came back to mentally irritate me. My stress got more serious after graduation. I still constantly researched case law surrounding my valedictorian dispute when I wasn't busy. Had the NYSED forced the NECSD to hand back my title, I wouldn't have felt like I had to do more research over the summer. In response to what I was going through, one person commented on social media, "Congratulations Matthew. I do realize the emotional trauma that you're going through, but this one can't be taken away from you. It's appalling that a board member's cell phone was used to contact [Newburgh's main newspaper] to try and defame you. There need to be changes made in that district and corrective actions put in place."

Given the seriousness of the data irregularities found in the grand jury report, you would expect corrective actions to also be put in place. You might recall that the NYSED announced they would audit the district, but as of the time of this book's publication, they have yet to release their findings. Many people I know, including my father, reached out to their spokespeople for an update on the investigation. None of them received a response. Because the State Education Department hasn't yet kept their word, people in my hometown started to feel as though no one could hold anyone accountable for the data obfuscation. I recorded interviews with several more teachers and administrators over the course of writing this book aside from the two who were featured in the third and fourth chapters. They are concerned about where the City of Newburgh is headed because they feel like the educational system is not getting enough support.

No one should ever feel like they're afraid, especially at school. Since June 2019, I haven't heard anything good coming out of Newburgh. My hometown's morale amongst the people I know has been completely destroyed, and there is great distrust between community members and the local institutions. Unlike what many experts (who usually don't even live in these impoverished neighborhoods) claim, cities like Newburgh aren't held back primarily because of general socioeconomic barriers. The Newburgh I know is held back because of the fear gripping the city.

As the social media user mentioned, there needs to be change within the public education system. During my spare time, I learned about a story coming out of the eighth largest school system in the country. They are based in Tampa, Florida (Hillsborough County), and their people overcame similar obstacles that poor communities like Newburgh face. I realized it was possible, despite all of the odds being against me, to overcome a burden.

Between 2012 and 2014, there were significant safety concerns in Hillsborough over how special needs children were being treated. The first safety incident made regional headlines after it was discovered that a seven year old girl died on a school bus. Her exact cause of death remains debated, yet her bus aides were not trained in CPR and did not call 911 when given the chance.[1] [2] News of the event encouraged several other families to file legal challenges against the district. The lawsuits cost the school district millions of dollars, degraded trust within public institutions, and led the BOE to fire its own superintendent.[3] [4]

There was a lot that I took away from this story. I read through all of the court depositions, watched dozens of news interviews, and looked at all of the websites/blog pages containing anything useful. I also managed to obtain police reports from the local sheriff's office and the last five evaluations that the school district used to evaluate its superintendent.

I initially requested this information because I wanted to know more about the superintendent who they fired. She just happened to be one of the NYSED officials who was presiding over my case, so I merely considered my work as important side-research. However, I came to an additional understanding that not all of Hillsborough's BOE members and administrators were happy about what was happening within their district. Like Newburgh, they wanted things to change for the better. By addressing safety concerns, everyone stood to benefit.

Unlike Newburgh, Hillsborough community members weren't afraid of voicing their views. Community organizers demonstrated outside of the board meetings for almost two years nonstop over the needs of special education children. I saw how these protests generated extensive news coverage and created a way for people to rally around their cause. Soon, BOE members sided with the protestors.[5] The depositions reveal that the open dialogue between school officials and parents led to necessary changes within how the school system operates. They created new emergency protocols, ensured the BOE would be immediately notified of when students get hurt, and worked with outside agencies to better reform the special education department. As the BOE members stood in the face of public criticism and dealt with lawsuits for the most serious charges that a school district could face, the school administrators didn't hide their faces. The BOE tried to be better, even while the problems kept coming.

This community really came together during a very difficult time and changed how people perceive the importance of special education. I admire Hillsborough for that level of bravery. They showed me exactly what this country needs to do more of if we are to truly fix school systems. Even though community members may be fearful of retaliation, they need to come out in full force at BOE meetings and BOE elections to keep demanding changes until those requests are granted. Don't worry about the potential consequences for voicing the truth. In the long run, failing to say anything is worse.

Those who write to the NYSED, such as the special education teacher who contacted the DA, exhibit similar qualities as Hillsborough's people. According to an op-ed which he later published, his experiences as a teacher showed him that many kids who graduated later had their futures jeopardized because they weren't educated and were left jobless in Newburgh.[6] They may not have been put in total life/death scenarios like the ones in Hillsborough, but they still went through life-altering crises. He wrote, "I was an active participant in that system and I sat by silently, avoiding confrontation, as the system destroyed one life after the other while patting itself on the back for its successes. I watched kids fall through the cracks that shouldn't have. I watched the system, time and time again, hand students a diploma while not giving them an education."[7] Yet after several years, he finally declared, "I could no longer participate in the process."[8] And through this righteous decision, he overcame his fear of avoiding confrontation with administrators.

Although there are many success stories of communities coming together and bringing positive change, we often don't hear about the consequences communities face when they don't unite.

My father's suffering during the summer after my senior year is the very thing that happens when a community does not come together. My dad was one of the people who wrote regularly to the NYSED. Some of the emails he wrote were related to political issues, but a vast majority of them were about his family. He wanted to be reassured that I would be well before I was expected to leave for college in 2019. Around that time, he felt like my entire undergraduate experience was in jeopardy because of a very weird report card I received in July. Entire classes and quarterly grades were just gone. A normal NFA report card contains all of the high school classes I've taken throughout the year during each academic quarter. My fourth-quarter grades and final exam scores in economics and English, however, were nowhere to be found. While you may recall from the previous chapter that information about my Government course appeared on my report card, this time, all of the grades from my government course were also omitted in their entirety. In the following figure, the circles indicate where some of the grades are missing. My dad wanted me to reach out to my friends from NFA Main and North to see if they had similar problems. None of them did.

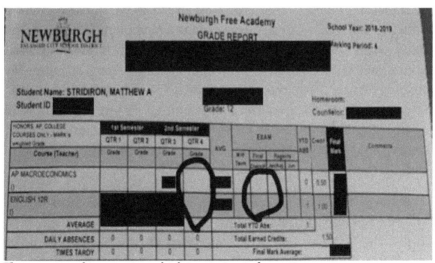

The report card in question which is missing information.

You might think this anomaly is no big deal at first. However, from his time on the BOE, my father knew that report cards are basically a mirror image of what your high school transcript looks like. That

SCHEMING IN THE DARK

transcript needed to prove I earned a certain number of credits in order to enroll at college. Right now, the report card did not reflect that I took a government class - a course needed to graduate in New York. While this may sound harsh, I technically couldn't register for classes in college without that credit because my university would think I didn't meet my graduation requirements. I was also getting emails about this from my university throughout July.

My father took this news very seriously. To alleviate my family's concerns, I emailed NFA's Guidance Office - the place where academic records are managed - and asked to review my transcript immediately. Their office had always been very accommodating and sent me what I needed by the end of the business day, even during the summer. This time, though, I learned through email that I wouldn't receive my transcript for quite some time. They alleged the transcripts weren't ready.

Ultimately, my family wrote a letter to the NYSED and waited it out for about a week. We didn't have to, but we wanted to be courteous in light of what they said. Under FERPA law, I'm entitled to get the transcript immediately. However after a week, my father wrote a letter to the BOE as a parent and made a passionate plea for help.[9] Emails were sent to the BOE for a whole month, turning what should have been an ordinary summer into a working vacation. My attorneys sent three more filings to the NYSED during the summer. A vast majority of the content, at one point, was just about more of the district's behavior. There was originally no expectation for me to write any more case filings given my part-time jobs, but I had to work on them with my lawyers.

What many may initially consider an anomaly in my records turned into another stressful, painful dispute. As we sent more information to the NYSED, I should also note that the NYSED could've forced the district to correct my grades, return my valedictorian title, and send accurate transcripts to my college at any time. The NYSED could've intervened whenever it wanted. Instead, my family didn't hear back from the department. We had to reach out to other parts of the New York State government, particularly its

Legislature, starting in June 2019. On June 3, my father commemorated my eighteenth birthday by emailing a freshman member of the New York State Assembly several case exhibits.[10] He responded within hours, and they arranged a time to talk over the phone. This wasn't the only time they communicated. Emails forwarded to me show the state congressman was contacted on July 12, July 15, July 31, August 6, and September 18.[11] By mid-July, he and his team of directors were horrified at what was going on. They didn't know how to respond, so they asked my father what they should do as professionals. One of the directors wrote, "I am stunned by the details of this case that continue to unfold. Is there any additional assistance that our office can be at this time, other than keep our contacts in [the] NYSED apprised of the updated details and the actions that you are seeking?"[12]

From the director's remarks, we know that the Assemblyman's staff notified other NYSED officials about what my family faced. Part of the NYSED's job is to look into fraud, waste, and abuse of power (FWA).[13] Their website claims "both the Board of Regents and the Commissioner of Education take these concerns very seriously."[14] The NYSED is required to conduct a preliminary assessment when they are contacted, according to their own website. The website is unclear about what that preliminary assessment entails, but it can result in one of three things: 1) an audit, 2) the complaint gets forwarded to a more appropriate agency, and 3) the case gets closed.[15] For example, the NYSED audited the district after the NECSD was caught altering attendance records. My father emailed the NYSED with case filings on June 3, July 12, July 31, September 13, and September 18, which required them to perform five preliminary assessments pertaining to the valedictorian dispute.[16] He told the state, "I want our schools to be the best-run schools ever. If data is continually manipulated, how can the real problems ever get addressed? *The stress and anxiety of this constant harassment are wearing me down. My health is in decline and I have no idea how long I can do this on my own. Newburgh needs someone to do something quick.*"[17] Knowing that my father was in distress, you might be asking whether the NYSED responded back to him to check on his health. We did not get any responses from them. We don't know whether they even conducted any of those preliminary reports.

In my father's opinion, it was one thing for the district to take a title from me. It was another thing for them to not restore omitted information from my records, which could prevent me from attending college. By mid-July, his mental and physical health rapidly deteriorated. To give you an idea of the stress he dealt with, I'm going to cite a complaint he wrote to a civil rights department.[18] My father wrote to them about Joey Johns' phone call to Newburgh's lead newspaper. Unlike the NYSED, the department did email him with two questions. He sent them an eleven-paragraph answer, three excerpts from my legal paperwork, and social media posts.[19] They didn't follow up with us, and he continued to suffer.

When my father didn't get a reply from the department, he reached out to other local officials. My father contacted one of the official's top aides on June 3, July 12, July 25, August 5, September 13, and September 18.[20] The September 13 letter is arguably my father's most emotional email. You can see him clearly signaling to his top aide that we needed assistance. *"We need your help. Please help."*[21] He didn't receive a response from the aide until this letter. The response reads, "The [official] and I are aware of the situation going on, I'm sorry to hear what you and your family are going through. Someone from my office should be reaching out to you today."[22] Unfortunately, my father never received a phone call.

To learn whether anyone in a position of authority responded to my dad's emails, I asked him to send me all of the emails regarding this matter from May 2019 to September 2019. What he sent me shows that none of the other state and federal bodies he communicated with gave him an answer. The only replies he received were from local officials, none of whom had any legal power to remedy this situation. Everyone who could have done something stayed quiet.

The key question I sought to answer that July was why the NYSED specifically did not publicly intervene when it could have either given a statement or ordered the district to support my family. The department was silent for over two months as members of my family were losing their minds. Throughout that entire summer, I had to be my family's defender. The number of hours I spent writing case filings in my basement reminded me of how much time I completed college applications seven months earlier. I filed a civil lawsuit with my father against the NECSD by mid-August, making my dad the first person in New York's history to sue both a school district and its BOE while actively serving on that same school board.

While my family is very well aware of life after high school, we all came to the same conclusion that what happened during the summer has made moving forward almost impossible. If you are in a position of power or in any position that is capable of helping someone who is losing their mind, you are required by law to intervene. All of these agencies and officials were more than capable of at least responding to emails. It's not like these officials were contacted once. You can see in the Google Drive that they were notified several times throughout the summer. They were very well aware of what was going on and chose not to do anything. Because the people of Newburgh chose to embrace silence as a solution to their problems as opposed to coming together like Hillsborough, this horrible situation arose where bad people hurt my dad.

This chapter is about one basic idea: resilience. Today, the people in Newburgh who feel threatened voluntarily accept to live in fear. A wall of silence has been created amongst the population so that the brave actions of any one person are ill-supported by their peers. When the Hillsborough community went through this similar period of fear, one of the board members argued, "It's very easy to step up to a microphone and say nice things about someone. It's very difficult, especially when you're afraid that you could be fired and you're afraid of some sort of retaliation, to step up and speak your truth."[23] Yet even though the school district went through one of the darkest times in its history, Newburgh and other parts of the country should look up to the response that Hillsborough took as an example for how to create more transparency within a community. As kids were getting hurt needlessly, the public was brave enough to go to the BOE meetings and have their voices heard. When they spoke out collectively, it became much harder to retaliate against any one individual because they were in a group. Ultimately, this forced change onto the district.

You may already be familiar with the idea of people getting disparaged immensely or even ousted from social life just for having a particular opinion. That idea is no different from other forms of retaliation because those people also have a fear of expressing their beliefs. Retaliation and fear are not uncommon in today's political climate. They have become the norm. Given that overcoming fear is a very difficult thing to do in today's world, overcoming it can very well define the next generation. I say this because of what happened to my dad. Retaliation is commonplace, and yet far too few people say anything about it either by choice or by fear. While he did not lose his physical life like the children, he did lose some of it mentally. He's not the same person anymore, and it's likely he'll never be the same. However, my father went above and beyond by putting himself on the line for me. In order to come after me, people had to come after my father first. If members of my local community were so submissive that they could not support my dad during the most harrowing time of his life from May to August 2019, especially after everything he's done as a BOE member for them, then Newburgh is heading down the wrong path.

I do believe that the individuals who failed to help my father do not represent the majority of the people who work at the institutions which they serve. They are probably filled with very fine people, yet there needs to be accountability for when these organizations fail to fulfill these basic obligations. After working with my attorneys, I was able to attend college in the fall and keep my scholarships because the NECSD returned my government course and its respective half-credit onto my academic records in mid-July. During the last few weeks of my summer vacation, my parents distracted me and they brought me out to several diners for breakfast and lunch. We went on five-to-six-hour shopping trips to get whatever I needed for school, or maybe just for the purpose of leaving the house. I had everything I needed well before the school's move-in day. Under normal circumstances, parents are proud but upset when their children leave home for college. I saw the social media stories of my friends who already left Newburgh, and they seemed extremely happy. As for my family, we all let out a sigh of relief instead. My summer "vacation" was finally over.

The road trip down from Newburgh to New York City was quiet. I remember leaving home thinking about everything I went through. The thoughts in my head were thankfully soon drowned out by the noise of sirens and honking vehicles found only in city life. University staff let us drive right into campus. Like all the other cars ahead of us, we were greeted with very loud, cheerful music and dozens of people waving at us. They had move-in bins ready for everyone, so I unloaded everything from my dad's truck and brought it to my dorm. Moving in took about an hour. Around lunchtime, many people ate lunch on the campus' two grass lawns while others continued to enter campus grounds for the first time. My parents found me sitting with someone who I met back at the school's pre-orientation, and he took pictures of my family and I before they left. This was the last time I planned to see them until Thanksgiving or Christmas. When I returned, I was expected to participate in my first legal deposition.

Confronting the events of the summer of 2019 is not only one of the bravest things I've ever done, but also a massive learning experience. This chapter, for me, was primarily about overcoming fear. Towns like Newburgh aren't just held back by socioeconomic barriers. They are held back by fear. Because they are held back by fear, institutions which directly influence the day to day lives of people (such as public education) have immense control over their constituents. I hope these chapters brought some level of justice for what the families of those children in Hillsborough went through. We mourn the loss of life. As someone who currently has a little brother about their age around the time of this book's publication, I have some understanding of why it's so important that we do everything we can to protect kids. I know that if Hillsborough could undo the damage brought to their community by voting in new people within these institutions, then so can any other part of the country. The only way that the government changes is through the power of your vote. The City of Newburgh will never get better if its people don't come together in the same way that Hillsborough did. They created such a large movement that they went to the polls, elected new people, and implemented policies that should serve as an inspiration to the rest of the country. To overcome life/death scenarios, fear, and mental health challenges, communities like Newburgh must mobilize similarly.

CHAPTER ENDNOTES

1   Marlene Sokol and Patty Ryan, "Parents blame Hillsborough school district for child's death after bus ride," *Tampa Bay Times*, November 1, 2012, https://www.tampabay.com/news/education/k12/parents-blame-hillsborough-school-district-for-childs-death-after-bus-ride/1259364/

2   Deposition of the Bus Driver, June 27, 2013, page 98, http://s3.amazonaws.com/assets.ollibean.com/wp-content/uploads/2014/04/28180400/Hillsborough-County-Public-School-Bus-Driver-Tonia-Dole-Pizarro-6.27.13-Deposition-Isabella-Herrera-Lawsuit.pdf

3   Marlene Sokol, "$800K deal reached over student who stopped breathing on bus (video)," *Tampa Bay Times*, March 26, 2014, https://www.tampabay.com/news/education/k12/hillsborough-ese-lawsuit-could-be-settled-for-800000/2172022/

4   ABC Action News, "Hillsborough schools superintendent terminated," January 20, 2015, Youtube video, 1:10, https://www.youtube.com/watch?v=yeMhAcNGzVk

5   Marlene Sokol, "Hillsborough School board members want to discuss issues surrounding student deaths," *Tampa Bay Times*, November 7, 2012, https://www.tampabay.com/news/education/k12/hillsborough-school-board-members-want-to-discuss-issues-surrounding/1260477/

6   Richard Desiderio, "I could no longer participate in the process," *Times Hudson Valley*, April 10, 2019, https://www.timeshudsonvalley.com/stories/i-could-no-longer-participate-in-the-process,5189

7   Ibid

8   Ibid

9   See Google Drive

10 Ibid

11   Ibid

12   Ibid

13   "Report Fraud, Waste, and Abuse," NYSED, http://www.oms.
     nysed.gov/oas/fraud/

14   Ibid

15   Ibid

16   See Google Drive

17   Ibid

18   Ibid

19   Ibid

20   Ibid

21   Ibid

22   Ibid

23   wmnfnews, "April Griffin on firing Hillsborough schools superin-
     tendent Elia 1: WMNF News," January 23, 2015, Youtube video,
     19:57, clip starts at 6:50, https://www.youtube.com/watch?v=Il-
     bCAkq_LU&t=969s

10
IMPARTIAL JUSTICE
JANUARY 2020

I f you type in Columbia University on any search engine, one of the buildings that you'll see has a figure of the Statue of Liberty sitting in a chair with a staff. Despite the text on the building that indicates it's a library, the structure itself is not a library anymore. It mostly holds administrative offices, but people usually sit by the steps all the time because of the view of campus. On the very first day I came back for my second semester in college, I sat up there for at least thirty minutes. From the steps, I could see the entire lower portion of the college and the small traces of snow that wouldn't be there for long. Below me were dozens of people greeting each other for the first time that year.

Although the school's academic calendar was divided into two semesters, it felt like one continuous year on my end. It began normally, yet a month into my first semester, the NECSD's attorneys at the Silverman & Associates Law Firm called in my entire family to speak in court depositions. We couldn't meet them due to some scheduling conflicts, so the attorneys moved these depositions to January. My family started out the new decade in a tiny room with a table. The district's attorneys sat across from us. One by one, we were interviewed. During my dad's deposition, I watched him testify against the district in a way that I don't think I will ever hear someone testify again. Not even the district's attorneys could hide the fear on their faces every time he mentioned the cruelty he endured. He spent over $15,000 in legal fees from June to January, and his business lost 72% of its business revenue while I was away because my father couldn't deal with the stress as he worked. In the most heartbreaking moments of the testimony, he cried. His wife was there to comfort him. I tried to offer him candy, but he refused. I looked across the table at the attorneys with such disdain.

My father used to be a very strong person. The news of his suffering surprised me because he always told me over the phone that everything was under control. In preparation for this deposition, he explained and cited hundreds of emails dating back six years to prove the retaliation against him by the school district. The attorneys had a huge folder containing all of this information in front of them because we were required by law to give it to them. We were also mandated to send them text messages, such as the ones involving Joey Johns' phone conversation, as well any crucial audio recordings like the one in "Searching for Answers." All of this evidence suggested that depriving me of my valedictorian title was part of a plot to seek vengeance against him. He talked to the attorneys for almost five hours, leaving them with no time to depose my mom. The next available time for her to testify was in late January, which meant I couldn't be present.

Back at college, everyone around me was filled with joy. Everyone but me, at least. During my free time, I researched previous valedictorian disputes that went to the NYSED Commissioner. The work impeded on days where I toured the city, met up with friends, and attempted to finish homework. One of these days was on the first Thursday of my second semester. I had a Friday class for which I needed a copy of my high school transcript, but it was still inaccurate. NFA had yet to update my final GPA from the Walking for Wellness course. Not knowing what the transcript would be used for, I texted my father.

"Should I ask [Newburgh Guidance] for the updated transcript?"

"No, just give them whatever you already have," he responded.

"Ok. It won't be accurate."

"You can bring [the valedictorian dispute] up in the comments if you want to. Is this a class discussion?"

"No idea."

"I bet your transcript would win with 'most interesting story.'"

"Certainly would."

"It would be interesting to hear what other smart people think about [the case]."

"If it comes up."

As I wrote back, I was researching a 1997 Newburgh co-valedictorian case. The Freedom of Information Act would allow me to access these public records as long as I contacted the NECSD's district clerk. I told my dad about the lawsuit quickly. Was it worth my time to ask the NECSD for the case documents?

"Wait, dad," I interrupted. "If we can FOIA emails, can we FOIA what happened in the case from 1997?"

"You can email [the district's clerk] and request the records. You would need to provide some details so that you can narrow the search."

"Ok. I'll do some side research before I choose to do anything."

Once this 1997 valedictorian dispute became public, it made big news. At the top of the second page of my search results was an article from the Education Weekly titled "Blind Student Says Class-Rank Flap Is Only Latest Indignity."[1] The dispute was also covered by the New York Times.[2]

"Do you know what the result was?" dad responded.

"No, not for the federal suit."

He found a ruling and sent me the URL.

"She lost in court. Our case has evidence."

"Reading it now. Can the NECSD decide to bring [our case] under a jury or judge?"

"I think defense gets to choose, but I am not certain."

"I worry they'll pay the judge off. I want to talk with [the student]."

On the very next day, the college's dining hall was empty when I got there. People were still sleeping following the Thursday night fraternity parties and city trips that extended well past midnight. Without a line, I got my breakfast and ate as fast as I could. In my hands was the Commissioner's verdict, but the ruling contained details about the dispute that would actually lead one to assume the Commissioner favored the valedictorian.[3] The student had the highest GPA out of the entire cohort in May 1997. However, the salutatorian's parents met with the district to possibly make her a co-valedictorian. According to the verdict, the BOE then publicly revised its class rank policy at the next board meeting to make the valedictorian become a co-valedictorian. How could the district just suddenly revise its class rank policy at the last minute in public? That's exactly what they did to me! None of it added up. Upon returning back to my dorm, I grabbed my audio recorder from a drawer and turned it on. I called up a relative of the supposed "co-valedictorian."

At the request of the relative, I will not disclose exactly what was said. Nonetheless, she seemed almost thrilled to talk about the case with a student who was going through the same thing as her family member. The person I interviewed is now in her early seventies. Even though we are separated by fifty years, we went through similar experiences within the Newburgh school system. She told me everything within half-an-hour. By the end of our call, I realized that this supposed 1997 "co-valedictorian" is actually a real valedictorian. Even more importantly, I realized that the dysfunction in Newburgh has been going on for the last sixty years - which helps explain why the city has been labeled dangerous for just as long. When the 1950-60s kids grew up in Newburgh, they lacked a good education. Their lack of knowledge left them skill-less after college, causing the city to deteriorate. As they raised their kids, they raised them in a school system full of people who hadn't been very well educated either. Once again, this made the city worse off because many kids couldn't succeed in college. Our intergenerational cycle of poverty will undoubtedly continue until something is done to break it.

The true 1997 valedictorian accomplished great things during her childhood, even while blind. Just like how I am one of the first P-TECH valedictorians, she is one of the first disabled valedictorians. Yet despite our achievements, we faced challenges just like those who struggle to get through high school. Although young, she too allegedly faced retaliation. Her family brought the district before the Commissioner of Education once she felt the administration stole her valedictorian title. Back then, the NYSED applied a "reasonableness" standard to determine whether the district's administrative decisions were improper.[4] The key question of this case was something along the lines of, "Did the NECSD BOE engage in improper behavior by publicly altering the class rank policy at the very last minute?" The Commissioner did what very few people would probably expect. In the decision, the 1997 Commissioner wrote, "Designation of a valedictorian or salutatorian is a local award for which reasonable standards may be imposed by a board of education. In this case, the board changed its academic recognition policy to enable it to acknowledge the academic achievement of the highest ranking student in its Regents program and the highest ranking student in its non-Regents program. I do not find this decision to be irrational or unreasonable." Not only did the Commissioner openly admit that the NECSD changed the policy at the last minute, but they also called it "reasonable." The higher courts then sided with this Commissioner and ultimately dismissed the valedictorian's case. No true justice was ever delivered.

I'm sure you also figured out the outcome of my case at the NYSED by now too. Over the fall, a new Commissioner (the one from the summer resigned) ruled in favor of the NECSD.[5] The NYSED was supposed to notify my attorney about the decision immediately, but they did not do so. We only heard about the news in advance because the BOE members rubbed the news in my dad's face. My dad told me that they all smirked at a private meeting and said to him, "We did nothing wrong." Akin to the 1997 decision where the Commissioner omitted much of what the relative told me, the new Commissioner omitted much of what you read in this book. The opinion was mostly based on district information which either had no evidence to support it or was based on information that I disproved in this book. Nonetheless, the Commissioner turned those false allegations into an official statement of fact.

No one should really be surprised by these 'rulings,' if you can even call it that, since the former Commissioner described in a letter how the NYSED planned to support the superintendent. What happened to the 1997 valedictorian can therefore happen to anyone. Unfortunately, my parents, siblings, and I will likely suffer a worse fate than her family's if no action is taken against the people who deprived my family of what should have been some of the happiest moments of our lives. Unlike the 1997 valedictorian, the NYSED caused my family to be in a desperate need of support. My youngest brother, who is currently six years old, has been diagnosed with autism and needs special care. I ended up talking with the relative about my brother for about one-sixth of our conversation because they could best relate to the situation we were in. The NECSD has a great program he could use, but we can't enroll him in the NECSD because of what happened to me. My father said in his deposition, "Newburgh has a great special education program, thanks in part to some of the work I've done as a member of the committees and the board. We have taken the special education system from noncompliance to compliance. And now I've gotten the system to this point, and we can't even use it. Now we have to move to another school system, another location. I have to move my business. All of my clients are here. I have to start from scratch at the age of fifty. That's ridiculous."[6] While you may believe that moving to a completely different city or state just so my brother can receive an education is overexaggerating my family's situation, it's not. He added, "I mean, just look at what they did to my son. Look at all the years I've been on the board and how much harassment I've dealt with. And because I was a witness in a grand jury that did the right thing, they took it out on my kids. That's one thing. I can handle it if you do stuff to me. But once you mess with someone's kids, no parent would ever allow that to happen. No parent would want to live in a property like that. We have a perfect piece of property. We looked long and hard for that property in the Town of Newburgh, where we can farm it, we can do everything we need to do. The kids love growing up there. For us to have to move at this point because of what happened from the school district is not fair. I should never have to go through this."[7]

It's hard for me to hear this from my father because I don't want to leave the home I grew up in. If there is a world where we can stay within the local area while my brother attends a different school, I'm sure my entire family would rather go down that path. However, my parents hardly have the money to do anything because the NECSD stressed my father out to the point where he lost a major income source! And once I learned about Hillsborough and those disabled children like my brother, I grew more frantic. Fearing my family would decline like others in the city for not getting the help they needed, I ultimately decided to write *Scheming In the Dark*. I did not write this book because of Newburgh's attendance problems. I did not write this book because of my valedictorian title. I wrote *Scheming In the Dark* solely for my father and my little brother. My entire family supported me. As I wrote up chapters, I wanted it to be about more than just me because so many other people have faced retaliation. I wanted it to save lives and shine such a bright light on the issues within school boards, state education departments, and courts that it would give people no choice but to really fight to reform the broken political and judicial systems we have in this country. The problems I wrote about can be found all over the United States, but there has not been a compelling story that would really motivate enough people to get out and fix the problems. In the eyes of many, my valedictorian story serves as that perfect catalyst for change.

As complex as the issues in this book are, some of them have very simple solutions. If there's one thing I could convince lawmakers to change across the country, I would ask them to bar their state education departments from offering official opinions on legal disputes. They are educational institutions, not independent judicial systems. Giving the Commissioner of Education the powers of a judge is outright absurd. Contrary to what you may expect, state education departments have a huge impact on national case law. Since the 1997 dispute, the true valedictorian's case has been cited over 111 times by judges in places like Vermont, Philadelphia, Arlington, and the District of Columbia![8] In addition, state education departments do not just rule on valedictorian cases. They decide all other state-related educational matters. We need to ensure there is greater organizational accountability among courtrooms and other institutions that impact the day-to-day lives of people. The idea of a fair justice system is enshrined in America's constitution, but when you find out you have to pay over $50,000 for a trial and competent attorneys, fairness suddenly gets a price tag most people cannot afford. Our justice system is geared in favor of the people who have political ties to courts. In my personal opinion, the groups that best promote accountability amongst the courts are whistleblowing protection agencies. Community groups and governments should collaborate to pass legislation that actually benefits whistleblowers, as well as fund independent agencies who can do a better job at protecting their clients from corporate, judicial, and government-led retaliation. One such example of legislation is a bill that creates term limits on elected officials like the BOE members. In towns of more than 30,000 people like Newburgh, board members should serve a maximum of three or four terms. Term limits impede corruption by opening our government to new people who have new ideas that can solve our country's greatest problems. Elected officials should also be recalled and voted out early if they are not serving the voters' interests. Some states have this already in place, yet other states don't.

Most of the people I know who are called "whistleblowers" do not consider themselves "whistleblowers." Being labeled as a "whistleblower" used to have a negative connotation attached to it. It seems, though, this perception is changing quickly because it is becoming more clear that the people who step forward are not trying to cause trouble. Now more than ever, as demonstrated in the last chapter, people across the country are voicing their concerns against injustices. I learned a lot more about myself within the two years since I started writing this book than in the other eighteen years I've been alive. It took superhuman strength to write this story. Originally, this book was 120,000 words. It took a very long time for me to get it down to under 60,000 words. My college years are supposed to be the best years of my life. While I certainly had fun working on this project, these years have been the worst. How would you like it if you had to relive the worst moments of your high school career every day throughout your entire undergraduate experience? That's exactly what I'm going through. During my college career, people saw what my family was going through, intentionally ignored our pain, and instead told me things like "It's no big deal." "Move on." "You're not going to have any problems." On the contrary, I experienced significant stress, anxiety, and irreparable harm to my undergraduate years, which is what the NYSED and the courts said there's no evidence for. I continued writing in my sophomore year at college. By the time this book gets published, I'll be at the end of my junior year. Despite how I attend a great institution, I spent so much time writing *Scheming In the Dark* that I wasn't able to spend my time at college where I needed to the most. As I have been focusing on my life and my family, everyone else at Columbia has been able to start building their careers. They're able to go on to graduate school or get a good job without worrying about anything holding them back. I'm happy for them, yet my future is uncertain. You've read about students whose lives have been damaged in Newburgh. I may have a reasonable chance of ending up like them.

On the same year that I talked with the relative, my father's 50th birthday came and passed. I asked him what he wanted as he blew out his birthday cake, and he said he wished for the judge in the civil court to return my valedictorian honor. This case touched every aspect of my dad's life, as well as my own. Since January 2020, I learned he spent another $15,000 on the civil case. We sent the judge twelve charges to review against the district. According to an email from my lawyer, she said the judge felt that the NECSD was

"either inept or there were some questionable things going on."⁹
The charges were definitely items that she would have to look into.
By August 2021, our attorneys sent us a phone number to a conference call the judge was holding. There, she deliberated which individual charges would move forward in civil court. The judge denied
my father his birthday wish. One by one, she dismissed them. She
only kept an assault charge and a violation of free speech charge.
The only reason she kept the latter charge is because the NECSD
didn't file anything to dismiss it. Although these two charges can
still force the district to return my valedictorian title as of the time
of this book's publication, I was disappointed. Here are the other
ten, evidence-based charges that the judge dismissed: negligence,
breach of fiduciary duty, breach of a non-delegable duty, fraudulent
concealment, intentional infliction of emotional distress, negligent
infliction of emotional distress, fraud, two 14th amendment violations, and slander. How does the judge go from calling the NECSD
"inept" to suddenly dismissing almost all the charges? I told my
dad that something probably happened. As she was in the middle
of dismissing the charges with my father attentively listening from
behind his desk, I came into his office and told him, "This case is
rigged!" I left the call mid-way through and continued editing my
book, which was about complete by that point. You would think
that the negligence charges would move forward without a problem. On the same day that the judge revealed her true intentions,
my dad emailed our attorneys his reaction. "The judge clearly stated
items were not shown as evidence, but we provided that evidence
to your office to back the claims. Anyway, the district was given
the green light by this judge to continue operating this way in the
future and they will be emboldened to do so."

The vast majority of the people who I talked with are convinced
that I proved my case beyond a reasonable doubt. In fact, my supporters are telling me that I uncovered a whole lot more about our
political system in general and deserve a second trial if this first trial
doesn't go in the peoples' favor. From what I know, we're entitled to
it. What they are also concerned about is the precedent this judge
created. If the courts are willing to let this behavior off the hook,

they're going to let public school systems get away with anything. That realization will have a much broader impact on the way education-related cases are decided, and it's something many people across the country are worried about. What if what happened to me happens to someone else? This judge made it possible for districts to get away with that.

Contrary to what you might think, my father did not stop his good work after hearing this news. In fact, I joined him. We encouraged more people to step forward. Despite everything that happened to him, my father ran and won re-election on the school board in 2020. He also decided to run again in 2022 because he will not be deterred from improving the lives of students. My family is not going to stop fighting for the things that my little brother and father need. People have told us that the only way they're ever going to trust the public education system and the courts again is if the district does the right thing and hands the title back too. Thankfully, the district will always have that choice. They can go into my transcript right now and update my final GPA from the Walking for Wellness course. Until then, their refusal to hand back the title only strengthens the need for judicial reform because the idea that the courts are non-partisan has been completely shattered. This is something that will affect school boards and courts for years.

I understand how easy it is for people to feel powerless and lost, but individuals have more power than they realize. When the government won't hold its own accountable, this book demonstrated that brave people who live in a free country will do so instead. At the end of the day, my hope is that some higher good will come out of all of this. There are people from all walks of life who are feeling pain or injustice, and I hope this book will enable everyone to get to a better place. *Scheming In the Dark* seeks to make our communities safer. Multiple teachers and administrators spoke with me for hours about their experiences and showed you, the reader, the importance of education and academic opportunities on breaking the intergenerational cycle of poverty. They shared the same goals as me because those goals are based on what is right. The things we believe in are things many of our readers would agree with too, yet not everyone is willing to say them publicly. I know that if we are able as a country to break that fear, we can bring judicial reform and impact the way we see local politics as it relates to state and national affairs.

For anyone interested in learning more about Newburgh, there is a second book you can purchase. It's called *Segregation of Minds*, and it was published by the 1997 valedictorian around 2015. On the front cover of the book is the Roman goddess Femida, who represents how far the courts still have to go before they truly deliver impartial rulings. While the 1997 valedictorian is blind and was home-schooled, I find it amazing how she was still able to get her story out in some form. I can recommend this book to be a good prequel. You can order the book from your local library for free or purchase it online. I ended up ordering it through Columbia. To this day, her book sits in Columbia University's Butler Library. It's a place that thousands of guests visit every week.

CHAPTER ENDNOTES

1   Caroline Hendrie, "Blind Student Says Class-Rank Flap Is Only Latest Indignity," *Education Weekly*, June 18, 1997, https://www. edweek.org/teaching-learning/blind-student-says-class-rank-flap-is-only-latest-indignity/1997/06

2   Evelyn Nieves, "Top Student Has to Share Top Honors," *New York Times*, June 1, 1997, https://www.nytimes.com/1997/06/01/nyregion/top-student-has-to-share-top-honors.html

3   Decision No. 13,946, New York State Education Department, May 26, 1998, http://www.counsel.nysed.gov/Decisions/volume37/d13946

4   Ibid

5   Decision No. 17,770, New York State Education Department, October 10, 2019, http://www.counsel.nysed.gov/Decisions/volume59/d17770

6   See Google Drive deposition, pages 132-133

7   Ibid, page 131

8   Court of Appeals for the Second Circuit, "Santina Polera, a Disabled Student, Plaintiff-Appellee-Cross-Appellant v. The Board of Education of the Newburgh Enlarged City School District, Defendant-Appellant-Cross-Appellee, William J. Swart, Individually and in His Capacity as Associate Superintendent, the Sarah N. Snowden Chapter of the National Honor Society, 288 F.3d 478 (2d Cir. 2002)," April 29, 2002, https://www.courtlistener.com/opinion/777468/santina-polera-a-disabled-student-plaintiff-appellee-cross-appellant-v/

9   See email in Google Drive. https://drive.google.com/drive/u/3/folders/1J4TU1coS3qi1jkmyhAs3VJ6HyGiZrQhv

POSTFACE

"Those of us who know, know. We knew exactly what it was as soon as it happened. Those of us who have been punished by the corrupt Newburgh machine can spot it from 10,000 miles away. Matthew Stridiron achieved the honor and prestige of becoming valedictorian of his graduating class, only to have it stripped away in a blatant act of retribution. It was retribution against his father, a school board member who caused too many problems and threw up too many roadblocks. That's how the machine viewed his father and that's why his son, despite having already received a letter congratulating him, had his moment robbed from him. He had worked hard for four years to achieve the distinction and worked extremely hard to maintain his lofty grade point average. The needs of the machine, the machine's ego, are all that matter in Newburgh. What you do, your achievements, do not matter, unless it feeds the beast.

So, he had his award stripped and was forced to share it with another student. "He still won." "It's not the end of the world." Those are both true statements that some have made, but both of those responses completely miss the bigger picture and the larger point. Matthew was denied an honor, for no other reason than for who his father was and is. The roadblocks that his father threw up against the administration of the Newburgh Enlarged City School District were done in service of children, none of whom were named Matthew Stridiron. He did what was right instead of going along to get along. Just like thousands of people have done over the years in Newburgh, he gave a voice to the voiceless. But that was not viewed favorably by the administration within the school district. Of course, I have no definitive proof that this conspiracy took place. Most conspiracies have no written or verbal evidence. They don't have a paper trail or recorded messages. If they did, they would be called crimes not conspiracies. That doesn't make them any less true. Those of us who know, know. I speak from experience. I went up against the entire machine. I know all too well the cost one pays for upsetting the proverbial apple cart. I have paid, and I have paid dearly. For an entire year, I reported all of the attendance malfeasance and corruption going on in Newburgh to the State Education Department. They did nothing. I was a witness in a grand jury investigation that centered around attendance fraud and the manufactured graduation rate in Newburgh. I was not hailed as a hero. I was harassed and denied advancement. I know the pain that sometimes comes with trying to do the right thing."

RICHARD DESIDERIO
former Newburgh Free Academy teacher

AUTHOR'S NOTE

Thank you for reading the entirety of *Scheming In the Dark*! I hope my book changed your perspective of how important local politics and courts are in regards to the larger picture of state and national affairs. I also hope that you'll become more involved in school board politics itself. You may have already decided to start attending your local board meetings, or maybe you decided to run for a seat on the BOE. Regardless of what you choose to do, always make your decisions with the best interest of the kids.

Please rate and review this book from wherever you purchased it from if you haven't already. Depending on where my future takes me, I may decide to write a second book. It would be great to know that I have your support.

RESOURCES

Some of my beta readers suggested that I put a list of resources together for anyone who wants to help my family. The past few years have been a very strenuous time for us, so we appreciate all of the support. You can:

Reach out to me at scheminginthedark@gmail.com with any individual tips or advice. News inquiries, however, should first attempt to reach out through my book website.

Contribute to my book's GoFundMe at scheminginthedark.com. I will try to use all proceeds to better my little brother's education, enable my family to move out of Newburgh, and fight my civil suit.

Follow *Scheming In the Dark's* Facebook page. Share the book trailer and our other posts on social media.

Bring attention to what my family is going through to journalists and media organizations. If you have an email list of journalists who I can reach out to, please forward it directly to schemlinginthedark@gmail.com.

Tell your local library and bookstore to house *Scheming In the Dark* and *Segregation of Minds* for other curious readers. Most of the time, all you need to do is call the local store branch over the phone.

Share news of this book with homeschooling and education groups on social media. Reach out to college book groups, fans of true crime novels, and those who study procedural justice.

People with information that could contribute to a second book should reach out to me as soon as possible. If *Scheming In the Dark* is to have a sequel, I would also prefer to work with a team of writers. Your name will be kept anonymous if you request it.

The NECSD's district clerk came up a few times in this book because he serves as a way for the public to get more information about legal disputes. You can officially request any additional documentation about the 2011 attendance problems, the 2019 grand jury investigation, the 2019 valedictorian dispute, the valedictorian dispute within Searching for Answers, and the 1997 valedictorian dispute at https://www.newburghschools.org/page.php?page=28

Given the unprecedented events that my family faced, *Scheming In the Dark* is one of the first books in history to disclose details about a legal dispute before an actual trial takes place. It is absolutely crucial that people from all of the states and nations who are reading this stand together and condemn the unjust actions led by the federal civil courts who are currently presiding over my case.

Local voters in New York should contact their representatives (usually through their website) and talk about my book. Additionally, ask them to fight for the legislative changes that *Scheming In the Dark* recommends.

Even if you do not live in New York, you can still contact your representatives.

- Here is a website to find your senator's contact information: https://www.senate.gov/general/contact_information/senators_cfm.cfm

- This one has your House of Representative member's contact information: https://ziplook.house.gov/htbin/findrep_house

- Here is a website to find contact information for your state governor: https://www.usa.gov/state-governor

- And here is one for state legislators: https://www.congress.gov/state-legislature-websites

Those who live outside the United States can follow similar steps as the one above.

Email the Newburgh City Council. They can improve the quality of Newburgh's education and the rights of whistleblowers through local legislation. They have an online contact form, which you can visit at https://www.cityofnewburgh-ny.gov/formcenter/Contact-Us-4/City-Council-Contact-Form-59

Ask the Orange County District Attorney's office to look into my case by emailing them at DistrictAttorney@orangecountygov.com. As of January 2022, the DA opened a second investigation into the NECSD over another separate issue. Like the 2019 investigation, a grand jury will be brought together to listen to witness testimony.

Request that the Newburgh BOE return my valedictorian title by emailing them at boemembers@necsd.net.

Contact the courts about my case by dialing their media/press-related phone number, as well as their main office phone number.

More information can be found here: https://www.nysd.uscourts.gov/about/directory

Email the NYSED's FWA program and ask them to fulfill its promise to complete the audit. Their website is here: https://www.oms.nysed.gov//oas/fraud/. Their email is FWA@nysed.gov.

You can also contact the NYSED's other branches for the same reasons. The Board of Regents, which works with the Commissioner on a regular basis, can be reached at RegentsOffice@nysed.gov.

CPSIA information can be obtained
at www.ICGtesting.com
Printed in the USA
BVHW082322050622
638965BV00007B/164